BRIGHT NOTES

FAUST BY JOHANN WOLFGANG VON GOETHE

Intelligent Education

Nashville, Tennessee

BRIGHT NOTES: Faust
www.BrightNotes.com

No part of this publication may be used or reproduced in any manner whatsoever without written permission, except in the case of brief quotations in critical articles and reviews. For permissions, contact Influence Publishers http://www.influencepublishers.com.

ISBN: 978-1-645422-68-6 (Paperback)
ISBN: 978-1-645422-69-3 (eBook)

Published in accordance with the U.S. Copyright Office Orphan Works and Mass Digitization report of the register of copyrights, June 2015.

Originally published by Monarch Press.
Paul Montgomery, 1963
2019 Edition published by Influence Publishers.

Interior design by Lapiz Digital Services. Cover Design by Thinkpen Designs.

Printed in the United States of America.

Library of Congress Cataloging-in-Publication Data forthcoming.
Names: Intelligent Education
Title: BRIGHT NOTES: Faust
Subject: STU004000 STUDY AIDS / Book Notes

CONTENTS

1)	Introduction to Johann Wolfgang Von Goethe	1
2)	Introduction to Faust	40
3)	Textual Analysis	
	Part One	53
	Part Two	114
4)	Character Analyses	154
5)	Critical Commentary	163
6)	Essay Questions and Answers	168
7)	Bibliography	172

INTRODUCTION TO JOHANN WOLFGANG VON GOETHE

PLACE OF BIRTH

Johann Wolfgang von Goethe was born on August 28, 1749, in the German town of Frankfort-on-the-Main. Family records indicate that his was a very difficult birth; Goethe later discovered that astrological signs had pointed to a late delivery and the possible death of the infant. Thus, the young Goethe's survival was considered remarkable. It was even a matter of some significance to the community as a whole, for his grandfather, a local magistrate, caused medical training to be extended in the town after seeing the difficulty his daughter was undergoing.

HIS PARENTS

Goethe's home life was happy enough, but his parents exhibited marked differences in temperament, and there was occasional strife between them. His father was a lawyer, as Johann himself was to be; he held a position of some civic importance, and took his career very seriously. His mother was very young when he was born; her disposition, according to her family's reports, was remarkably sunny. Some biographers have noted, however, that she resented her husband's concern with civic affairs, often felt lonely at home, and, as Johann grew older, leaned on him more and more for companionship.

EARLY MEMORIES

Goethe's reminiscences are filled with his attempts to recapture his very earliest memories. He knew that an adult often mistakes what he has been told for what he actually remembers, and he tried very hard to sort out the truth from the secondhand material; the memories of childhood were of great importance to Goethe. What seemed first to penetrate his consciousness was an awareness of the great, old house that he and his family inhabited in Frankfort. His description of this house makes it sound like a medieval castle: "Stairs as in a tower led to originally unrelated rooms, and steps were needed to connect the storeys … at the door there was a tall grillwork … like a great cage." If the house sounds bizarre to the child of the efficient, split-level ranch, it was a haven to the imaginative young Goethe. He and his beloved younger sister Cornelia found unexpected corners all over the house, and played for hours uninterrupted by adults. Goethe also loved to watch the activity in the back yard, where the neighborhood women performed their household tasks.

FAMILY

Although there were only two children, Cornelia and Johann (five others died very young), the family establishment was rather a large one. There were Johann's parents, his grandfather and grandmother, several servants, and, as guests, many of the more prominent men of the day. They were not an ordinary family: his grandfather was an interpreter of dreams and a prophet of sorts; his mother was an inventor and teller of fairy tales; his father was extremely fond of maps, and often planned imaginary journeys with the family. The great sensitivity, the awareness of a mystical other world, soon made itself felt in both children, and Cornelia and Johann were delighted with all kinds of imaginative play.

Johann, however, was a "strange" child even in this rather extraordinary family. From the very first he was repelled by all ugliness; a note in his mother's memoirs indicates that he refused, when only three, to play with another child who was slightly deformed. Johann was upset for hours about the "ugly" child, and seemed to resent the presence of any ugliness in the world. The young Goethe apparently realized his own difference. He was often teased for his unchildlike dignity, but he answered that he would "distinguish himself" somehow when he grew older, and so must set himself apart now.

ROMANTIC ENTANGLEMENT

From his very earliest youth, Goethe was a highly sensitive, volatile, emotional person. The three-year-old who cried at ugliness and insisted on personal dignity might seem ridiculous; however, it is this intense awareness of self and others which eventually produced the poet Goethe. His turbulent nature and his tendency toward romantic attachments made themselves evident very early. When he was still in his teens he had fallen in love violently several times. Each new love inspired in him the greatest extremes of emotion; his notes and letters from this period are filled with violent despair and the heights of elation. After one of these emotional periods was over, however, even the teen-aged Goethe could reflect objectively on himself and his own behavior. Invariably, he felt himself drawn back to his home and his family, which to him represented order and establishment in a hectic world.

GOETHE AS STUDENT

The young Goethe attended school first in Frankfort, then in Leipzig, where he studied law and led an active social life. He was as unusual a young man as he was a child, however, and comments by his friends indicate that he was loved by some and detested by others. He was described as a vain young man, well aware of his considerable physical appeal and of his talent at poetry. His friends realized his talent and charm. His enemies, however, simply considered him an overbearing, conceited fool. Eventually the young man's rebelliousness seemed to overcome his desire for social acceptance; by the time he is seventeen one finds him writing in his diary about the reasons why the "best" families of Leipzig had dropped him from their visiting lists. Goethe himself realized that he often appeared pedantic and smug; as an older man he seemed amused and unrepentant about his childhood escapades and his outspoken criticisms of friends and of society in general. Though he eventually commanded the respect of the entire literary world, he never became a conformist.

ILLNESS

The high living in Leipzig came to a sudden and violent end, however. Goethe was overcome in 1768 with severe hemorrhaging, and was confined to bed for several weeks before going home for nearly two years of convalescence. Reports of these two years at home are not pleasant; his father, who had grown morose over setbacks in his career and over the deaths of several members of the family, now fastened all his hopes on young Johann. There was strife between his parents, and Johann himself was emotionally disturbed by the life he had been leading in Leipzig.

STUDY IN STRASBOURG

After the lengthy period of unhappy convalescence, young Goethe went on to the University of Strasbourg, where he finished his legal studies. Here again he made romantic conquests and many friends. One of the more significant acquaintances from this time of his life was the German writer Johann Gottfried von Herder, one of the most prominent of the early Romantic writers. Herder has been credited with inspiring Goethe's first really serious poetic creations. Goethe himself has often mentioned the marked effect which Herder's friendship had on him; he states in his memoirs that he never could destroy a single word Herder had written to him, "not even the address on the envelope" of his letters.

FRIEDERIKE BRION

The year 1770 marks the beginning of a short, idyllic period in Goethe's life. He had been working hard on his poetry (inspired at least in part by the ideas and writing of Herder), and, in an attempt to rest after his studies and literary work, he often left Strasbourg for neighboring towns. In one of them, Sesenheim, he met Friederike Brion, the daughter of a pastor. Goethe's love for Friederike stands out in the midst of all his other romantic alliances; this affair, far from being emotional and turbulent, was peaceful, idyllic, and, apparently, inspiring. Eventually, as he so often did, he grew tired of the girl and broke off the relationship. The months in Sesenheim remained with him, however, as a peaceful period in the "storm and stress" that was his early life.

LITERARY FAME

After leaving Strasbourg Goethe went back to Frankfort, where he practiced law and did some writing. In 1773 his first real literary fame came with the appearance of his drama, Gotz von Berlichingen; the next year he achieved even more notice with the publication of his novel *The Sorrows of Young Werther*. He also wrote many poems during these years, and, as usual, courted several young women. Among his writings were critical pieces for newspapers, though these were not his greatest successes- he was often accused of mocking rather than criticizing.

HIS CAREER IN WEIMAR

In 1775 Goethe went to Weimar at the invitation of the young Duke Charles Augustus of Saxe-Weimar. It was the city of Weimar that was to be Goethe's home from that year until his death, except for some rather brief journeys to other parts of Europe. In Weimar he pursued a highly successful political career as well as a literary one, holding various positions of state under the Duke, his patron. He served for a time as prime minister, and in 1782 was made a nobleman. Eventually, however, he found these political duties-and several romantic attachments-too exhausting, and in 1786, eleven years after he came to Weimar, he went to Italy for an extended visit.

CHARLOTTE VON STEIN

One of the reasons for Goethe's retreat from Weimar was his love of Charlotte von Stein, a married woman and the mother of several children. Their relationship at first was simply friendship, a meeting of similar minds; eventually, however, Goethe realized that he could not be satisfied with this. Rather than destroy the relationship entirely, he decided to leave for a time. Charlotte von Stein is credited with having had an excellent influence on the young writer, both in his life and in his writings, and this relationship is considered to be one of the most influential ones of his life. It is generally accepted that the love poetry of this period is fuller, more mature and controlled, than that which had been written before, and the influence of Frau Stein is generally given as the reason. One biographer, Emil Ludwig, calls Frau Stein the "harder diamond which could grind down Goethe's angles."

ITALY

Goethe was struck by the beauties of Italy-the sun, the light, the mountains, the sea-everything entranced him. He said he felt like an exile returning to his home; though he had never before been to Italy, it was as if he had been intended for that place. He steeped himself in Italian art, culture, and scenery for nearly two years. His amusements were varied and simple-he took walking tours, painted, and enjoyed himself with a small group of friends. He thoroughly enjoyed the relaxation of the political and emotional tensions under which he had been laboring in Weimar.

LITERARY SIGNIFICANCE

This trip to Italy is most important in any evaluation of Goethe's literature, for it was here that he first encountered the order, restraint, simplicity, and emphasis on form which mark Classical art. These ideals influenced everything that he wrote after this time, and tempered the emotional and romantic content of his work.

WEIMAR AGAIN

After two years in Italy Goethe went back to Weimar, where he took up his old friends and interests. He formed another romantic attachment, this time with the very young Christiane Vulpius. Contemporary comment indicates that Christiane was quite the opposite of Charlotte von Stein; she was a childlike, simple young woman, not at all the intellectual. Goethe's feeling for her was strong, however, and this alliance lasted much longer than most of his others had. She bore him a son, and this event seemed to deepen Goethe's emotional life; in 1806 he married Christiane, nineteen years after she had become his mistress.

SCIENTIFIC ENDEAVORS

During this period in Weimar, Goethe pursued what was a second, but very strong, interest: he worked on scientific experiments and wrote articles on the results. His letters from this time indicate that he was somewhat disillusioned with Germany, after his Italian visit, and with his writing, which had become unusually difficult for him. His interest in science, and some critical remarks about Germany, furthered that isolation from society which had been evident from childhood days. Goethe took to spending more time alone or with his growing family; and he became more and more a religious and social skeptic.

FRIEDRICH VON SCHILLER

It was in Goethe's middle years, 1794, that he formed another extremely significant friendship. This was with the German poet Friedrich von Schiller, who had a marked effect on Goethe's poetry. Goethe, whose letters and diaries from this time indicate that he was losing much of his poetic inspiration, was remarkably impressed by the younger man. And Schiller had long been fascinated by stories of the eccentric Goethe. Their friendship grew slowly, because of Goethe's reluctance to join society, but the two men eventually became very close. Both were emotional and high-strung; they disagreed often and sometimes violently, yet the personal impact of their friendship was seen in the writings of both.

ILLNESS AGAIN

In 1806 Goethe again suffered a severe illness. He recovered and began writing again, but withdrew increasingly from society. Some of his best poetry was written during these later years. Among other things, he continued to work on *Faust*, which, though begun early (1769), was not finished until shortly before his death in 1832. In 1808 the first part of the tragedy as we know it was published; Goethe was never really satisfied with the remainder, however, and it was not published until a year after his death.

VISIT WITH NAPOLEON

While working on *Faust*, Goethe had maintained his interest in philosophy and in current affairs. Napoleon, who in 1808 was at the peak of his fame, was a man who fascinated Goethe and when the Frenchman visited Germany, Goethe eventually had an audience with him. It was at this historic meeting that Napoleon, looking at Goethe, simply exclaimed, "There is a man!" Napoleon greatly admired the German; against Goethe's modest disclaimers, he considered him the greatest German dramatic poet of the time. The two men saw much of each other during Napoleon's stay, and Goethe, who was now sixty years old, became a figure of major national importance once again.

THE LAST YEARS

Goethe's last years were a time of great spiritual pain. Deaths in the family and deaths of friends made his old age lonely, and his letters and diaries of this time indicate that he suffered greatly from this loneliness. Nevertheless he kept working, revising *Faust* until a few days before his death. His last days were painful indeed; he lingered in great illness until he died, at home with his family, on March 20, 1832.

Goethe had been a controversial figure during his entire lifetime. He inspired both hatred and devotion; no one who knew the man seemed able to feel neutral about him. He has been praised for his unrelenting search for truth and beauty, and damned for egotism, selfishness, and disregard for the feelings of others. Whatever his personality, however, he certainly was, in Napoleon's words, "a man"-a man of the greatest complexity and the most towering talent.

INFLUENCES

Those influences which affect a creative artist cannot really be listed definitively-the whole world, the spirit of the times, the personality of the artist himself obviously become a part of the material he creates. In the case of every individual, however, there are certain influences, more obvious and direct than others, which can profitably be observed. The strongest influences are usually the simplest-family, friends, education, reading. Goethe was no exception. A look at his diaries, his letters, his memoirs and those of his friends, gives a good picture of those people and situations which he most reacted to in his life, and which are most evident in his writings.

His Father

Nearly all Goethe's comments about his father are tinged with a subdued and controlled bitterness. Johann Caspar Goethe was an interesting and impressive man in his own right, but he was a stern perfectionist, and expected of his son the same kind of accomplishments as he had achieved. The fact that five of his seven children had died aggravated young Johann's situation, since his father fastened all his hopes on his one son. Even before he was in his teens Johann realized this; in his autobiography one finds him reflecting, "I was to go the same way as father, only farther." Add to this the frequent periods of gloom which plagued his father, and one can understand why the young man often resented him.

Choice Of Vocation

Johann Caspar Goethe's perfectionism and insistence on control were most evident in the education which he mapped out for his son and daughter. The two were taught primarily by tutors during their early youth. When the time came for choosing a career, young Johann was sent to Leipzig to study law as his father had, much against his own wishes. Johann's comments from this time, and those of his friends, indicate that this was at least partially responsible for his intemperance and his foppishness at law school; he found the courses tedious and strenuous, and his imprudent life was, in part, a rebellion against being too strictly controlled.

His Mother

If Johann Caspar Goethe was gloomy and embittered, his wife, Katharina Elisabeth, was quite the opposite. She was only eighteen when Johann was born, closer in age to her son than she was to her husband. The general opinion of their contemporaries is as positive about Katharina as it is negative about her husband; all reports agree that she was extraordinarily lively, charming, intelligent, and cheerful. She formed the balance in Johann's youth: her inveterate gaiety tempered the father's gloom, her cheerful, loving nature tempered his harsh, strict one. She was also a highly intelligent woman, and from the start satisfied Johann's desire for a life of the imagination. She would make up fantastic fairy tales, or tell stories of historical incidents by the hour. Her aptitude for languages also influenced her talented son, who eventually became fluent in seven languages; his earliest schooling familiarized him with the literature of many different nations.

Strife

The contrast between the personalities of Goethe's parents caused unhappiness in their home, an unhappiness of which Goethe was aware even when still a child. He knew his mother was often bored and unsatisfied with the quiet routine of the housewife; he knew that his father was often gloomy and uncommunicative; he knew that his mother used him as an outlet for her imagination. Loving his mother as he did, he could not help resenting his father for the part he played in her unhappiness. The situation grew critical after Goethe became ill and returned from his studies in Leipzig. His father had had recent setbacks in his own career, and was enraged when his son seemed to be an an invalid and a failure. His mother, who had been even lonelier with her son gone, was all the more loving and possessive when he returned home ill.

Results

A distressing home life, of course, is certainly no rarity, and thousands have overcome the handicap that it imposes. To Goethe's sensitive nature, however, it was a constant aggravation. The discord made him aware from his earliest days of the unhappiness and pain which could be caused by different personalities in close contact. His father's strictness and insistence on a legal career heightened his rebelliousness and his tendency to withdraw from close relationship. On the more positive side, of course, this situation made him more aware of the psychology of women than he might otherwise have been. Much of Goethe's skill in creating feminine characters has been attributed to his affection for his mother. On the whole, the effect of his discordant home was to heighten his sensitivity.

Education

Even Goethe realized that his father had contributed one very valuable gift-a broad and highly sophisticated education. The Goethe home was filled with books, and Goethe was reading, before his teens, many books which are unfamiliar to today's college graduates. One of his early favorites was the Acerra Philologica, a collection of fables, mythologies, and fantastic tales gathered from all over the world. These stories, which he read avidly, nourished the boy's appetite for the fantastic and the imaginative.

He also read imaginative books of travel; his father's love of travel encouraged him in this, and his favorites included *Robinson Crusoe, Island of Felsenburg*, and *Journey Round the World*. As he grew older he increased his reading of the classics: Ovid's *Metamorphoses* was one of his first friends. He came to Homer as a teenager, and devoured *The Iliad* and *The Odyssey*. When Goethe was dissatisfied with the ending of *The Iliad*, a professor sent him to Vergil. The Latin poet remained a favorite writer throughout his life.

This familiarity with the classic in itself exerted an obviously beneficial influence on the beginning poet. It had a second effect on Goethe, however: it made him long to see Italy, and increased his receptivity to that country when he eventually traveled there. The classical elements of his post-1788 writing did not simply materialize out of thin air; he had been a lover of classicism from his earliest youth.

One more reading favorite deserves mention-Torquato Tasso, the Italian pastoral poet of the sixteenth century. Tasso captured Goethe's imagination immediately, and he always remained fascinated. One of Goethe's more famous plays deals with the life of this man; in the play it becomes clear that Goethe saw significant parallels between the Italian's career and his own.

Religion

The Bible was very important to Goethe. His earliest reading was in this book, and he never lost his love of the Scriptures. He was impressed, of course, by its literary excellence, but he also found it a source of continuing spiritual inspiration. Goethe was a questioner rather than a believer from the very first, but the Bible remained a constant part of his life. His belief always centered around it.

First Doubts

Goethe's autobiography indicates that he was only six when he first began to have doubts about the traditional Christian concept of God. The Lisbon earthquake, which occurred in 1775, was both literally and figuratively earth-shaking. It was a disaster of unparalleled magnitude, killing thousands of people and causing immeasurable damage to property. Also the earthquake was seized on by preachers all over Europe, and, in a revivalistic series of sermons, a "hellfire and brimstone" God was preached for months. Goethe's autobiographical account of his reaction is somewhat amusing-he was, after all, only six years old and a bit young for serious theological thought. But it is also significant, for the earth quake and the sermons made him wonder about the goodness of God and emphasized in his young mind the wrathful Jehovah of the Old Testament. Johann had always been afraid of violent storms, and after the earthquake he expected the end of the world every time there was a thunderstorm. This kind of serious meditation on God seems incredible in so young a child, but Goethe was hardly an ordinary boy, and by the time he was in his teens, he was a thorough skeptic.

His Religious Environment

The peculiar quality of the religious world in Germany during Goethe's youth did nothing to help his doubts. Religion was beset by internal quarrels and unable to resolve the major questions of the day. As a teenager Goethe commented on the divisive, quarreling Protestantism that he knew: he called it a "dry morality," appealing only to the intellect and condemning the senses. He had great respect for organized religion-his mother and many of his friends were faithful churchgoers-but it is inconceivable that the emotional, imaginative, sensitive young Goethe could have accepted for long the sects he saw around him.

The Personal God Of Nature

Goethe, who asked religious questions all his life, never really found an answer. During most of his young manhood he found a god in the spirit of nature; for years this spirit of nature was for him the most satisfactory kind of deity. As an old man his autobiography indicates that he "found a Christianity for private use," built primarily on the Bible, his scientific knowledge, and his love and knowledge of the natural world. He never ceased believing in a god, but he was too much the individual, too much the rebel, too much aware of the value of the senses, to accept the orthodox religious beliefs which he saw practiced by the people around him.

Herder

Besides the usual influences of family life, education, and the search for religious belief, several outstanding friendships affected Goethe's life considerably. The first was with Johann Gottfried von Herder, whom Goethe met while a student at the University of Strasbourg. Through Herder, who was older and had already done a good deal of writing, Goethe met many of the young intellectuals of Germany. He also encountered the romantic ideas of Jean Jacques Rousseau, one of the most influential writers in the history of literature.

Herder has been called the founder of Sturm und Drang (storm and stress), a movement that sought to free literature from domination by neoclassicism. Like Wordsworth in English poetry, Herder rebelled against the strictures of the previous literary age. He opened the windows in German writing, emphasizing the spirit and the language of the common people rather than the artificiality of the upper classes. He pointed to folk material and to the Bible as examples of truly living, significant literature. Herder's thought and his critical writings inspired Goethe in his own creation. Herder also reintroduced him to the best of Greek literature, and to Shakespeare. Goethe had read Shakespeare before this time but not seriously; after Herder's treatment, however, the great English dramatist became a major influence in Goethe's writing.

Schiller

A second inspiring and significant friendship occurred much later in Goethe's life. His relationship with Johann Christoph Friedrich von Schiller was a tumultuous but most influential one. At first the older Goethe "detested" what he read of Schiller's writing. Recently returned from Italy and disenchanted with much of German culture, Goethe felt that Schiller exemplified all that was worst in German writing, including his own. He considered him emotional, immature, formless, unpolished, and avoided any contact with him. Goethe was then having difficulties with his own poetry, and for a time gave it up almost completely to pursue his scientific writing. Eventually, however, he and Schiller met, in 1794. The initiative had been Schiller's; he asked Goethe to contribute to *The Hours*, a magazine he was editing. Goethe accepted the invitation, and thus began a friendship which lasted until Schiller's death in 1805.

Second Spring

The two men continued to disagree throughout their friendship, but their differences were amiable after they had thoroughly discussed their ideas. Goethe considered that Schiller had "rescued" him from science, enabling him to recover the joy in poetry which he had lost. Schiller also introduced his friend to the most important philosophical ideas of the day, notably those of Immanuel Kant, the German philosopher who so strongly influenced Romantic thought.

The personal relationship between the two men was also important, for Goethe found in his friend an enthusiasm for his writings and his ideas which had been lacking in his life for some time. It was indeed a "second spring" for him, as he says in his autobiography, and his writings show the good effect of Schiller's new philosophical thought and his enthusiasm.

ROMANTICISM

Romanticism was so important an influence on *Faust*, and indeed on almost all Goethe's work, that it merits separate discussion.

Introduction

Romanticism must be considered in two ways: as a way of approaching reality and as an historical movement with discernible beginnings and concerns. One might define the ahistorical or perennial romantic as a man who is dissatisfied with the present state of things. He is dissatisfied with imperfection and limitation in himself and the world around him, and this dissatisfaction causes him either to try to transform himself and the world, or to try to escape to a better world. Like Ulysses, he quests for the transforming experience; or like Plato, he tries to formulate a perfect society; or like the religious mystic, he strives to escape from this imperfect world by linking himself to a transcendent being.

Historical Romanticism—The Term

The adjective "romantic" was derived from the Old French *romant* or *romanz* meaning a romance or romantic story. As an adjective it first appeared in English about the middle of the seventeenth century. In its first usages it meant "like a romance," which at the time had the pejorative **connotation** of fanciful, improbable, illusory, or unreal. By the middle of the eighteenth century, "romantic" lost its pejorative **connotation** and became associated with things that were imaginative, and nature that was pleasantly melancholy. As English nature poetry-notably James Thomson's *The Seasons*-was translated into German, the new English **connotations** of the word were absorbed by the German word romantisch. In France the new senses of the word were attached to romantique, a word which gained in popularity among writers toward the end of the century.

First Critical Use

It was not until the very end of the eighteenth century, however, that "romantic" was used as a critical term. A German critic, Friedrich Schlegel, first used the term in contrast to "classical." Mme. de Stael helped popularize this use of the term in her *De l'Allemagne*, a work written in 1810 in which she praised German poetry for being "romantic." The popularization was continued in England with the translation in 1815 of A. W. Schlegel's *Dramatic Art and Literature*, a series of lectures on Shakespeare and Calderon. "Romantic" as a term designating discernible literary tendencies was firmly established through use by nineteenth century English writers such as Coleridge and Carlyle.

Rousseau

Although romanticism cannot be reduced to Rousseau, he is, if not the Father of romanticism, one of the most luminous and informing figures of the movement. Born in Geneva on June 28, 1712, the French writer spent the first 37 years of his life traveling about the continent, holding a variety of positions ranging from music teacher to servant. The turning point in his life, and one of the landmarks in the history of the Romantic Movement, occurred in 1749 when he entered an essay contest being held by the Dijon academy. The topic was phrased as a question: Had the advance of the sciences and arts helped to destroy or purify moral standards? In his prize-winning answer Rousseau began to formulate the main tenets of what was to become known as the Romantic Movement. His answer, which attacked intellectual order and which emphasized the emotional side of man, was that the sciences and arts had always been harmful to morality because they undermined the natural virtue of the human heart. This revolt from the intellectual standards of eighteenth-century rationalism continued in successive works. In *Concerning the Origin of Inequality Among Men* (1754), he asserted that man in his original, uncivilized state is innocent, placing the responsibility for man's corruption on society. Thus, Rousseau inspired and gave impetus to the idea of the "noble savage," an idea which was to grip the imagination of the Western world for the next 200 years.

In *Julie, or the New Heloise* (1761), Rousseau emphasized the importance of intuition and the inner man in an ideal love relationship. In *The Social Contract* (1762), he advocated a community of free men who freely subordinate their wills to the will of the majority. In *Emile* (1762), he reaffirmed his belief in the naturally good man, arguing that if a child is allowed to develop naturally, away from the corrupting influence of society, he will be a good man.

In the *Confessions* (1765–1770), he treated the uniqueness of man, the dignity of the individual, and the value of the emotions in personal relationships. "I am commencing an undertaking," wrote Rousseau in the *Confessions*, "hitherto without precedent, and which will never find an imitator. I desire to set before my fellows the likeness of a man in all truth of nature, and that man myself." The implications of the opening sentence were far-reaching. Rousseau was announcing the value of all human actions, and was doing so in an intensely personal and egotistical way. The confession, thus established by Rousseau, was to become the essential mode of expression for later romantic writers.

The Pre-Romantic Movement

The same spirit which informed the writings of Rousseau during the third quarter of the eighteenth century produced in England a rich pre-romantic literature predating Rousseau's landmark essay of 1750 by 41 years; In 1709, an influential English thinker, Anthony Ashley Cooper, Third Earl of Shaftesbury, created a romantic undercurrent in the flood of neo-classic literature by stressing the importance of man's emotional nature. Shaftesbury (as he is commonly known) began to undermine the neo-classic standard which identified moral progress with progress in education by suggesting in *An Inquiry Concerning Virtue or Merit* (1709), that man's moral sense was not improved but corrupted by education. He foreshadowed Rousseau by identifying man's moral sense with emotion rather than intellect; this foreshadowing continued in *The Moralists: A Rhapsody* (1711), in which he proposed a natural religion. Such a religion would have the natural world for its setting and would allow man to make full emotional response to God.

Nature Poetry

The publication of James Thomson's *The Seasons* during the second quarter of the eighteenth century signaled a new awareness of nature in English poetry. This awareness, to become one of the identifying characteristics of nineteenth-century romantic poetry, can be found in the closeness with which the poet observes nature and in the delight taken in such observation. Thomson, like Shaftesbury and Rousseau, also endowed nature with a religious significance. "Oh talk of Him in solitary glooms," begins a key passage in the concluding portion of *The Seasons*, "Where o'er the rock the scarcely waving pine/Fills the brown shade with a religious awe." It was the translation of this poem which established in Germany the English **connotations** of "romantic."

Graveyard Poetry

The second quarter of the eighteenth century also saw the rise of a poetry of melancholy and death. Robert Blair's poem *The Grave* (1743), in which the speaker luxuriates in the thought of death, gave this type of poetry its name. Two of the better poems which continued this indulgence of melancholy as an emotion were Edward Young's *Night Thoughts* (1742–44) and Joseph Warton's The *Pleasures of Melancholy* (1747). "Tired nature's sweet restorer, balmy Sleep!" croons the speaker of "Night Thoughts" at the beginning of a passage lamenting the suffering man must endure in this world. "I wake," concludes the speaker, "how happy they who wake no more!" One of the most striking romantic features of this pre-romantic poetry is the degree to which the speaker was alienated. He was almost always represented as the solitary man acutely aware of, and lamenting the limitations of man while feeling a strong desire for death as an escape from a life which has become an agony.

Poetry And The Past

Another romantic tendency found in eighteenth-century England was the interest in the past. The past, particularly the Middle Ages, attracted writers with a romantic temperament since it was the complete opposite of neo-classicism. It represented mystery, emotion, imagination-terms foreign to an age which identified man with reason and which saw the world as a machine with a perfectly predictable order. Two works inspired new interest in the past: James Macpherson's *Ossian* (1760–63) and Thomas Percy's *Reliques* (1765).

Ossian

Between 1760 and 1763, James Macpherson published a group of poems which he claimed to be translations of works by a medieval Gaelic poet called Ossian. Ossian soon became a famous name, and the volumes published by Macpherson under that name inspired writers who were beginning to formulate romantic theories concerning the nature of man and civilization. Thomas Gray, an influential poet who wrote **Elegy** in a Country Churchyard, was attracted to the imaginative descriptions of nature which the poem contained.

Other romantic writers were drawn to Ossian's heroes, who appeared to be proof of Rousseau's theory of the "noble savage." These heroes, although living in a primitive society, were naturally well-mannered, sensitive, and generous. They also responded to the world emotionally rather than intellectually. "The sons of song are gone to rest," laments Ossian with an indulgence of emotion similar to that of the Graveyard Poets. "My voice remains, like a blast that roars lonely on a sea-surrounded rock, after the winds are laid. The dark moss whistles there; the distant mariner sees the waving trees!" Today, the Ossian poems are accepted as a hoax; Macpherson, a man attuned to the times, had simply designed them to appeal to the growing number of people who were dissatisfied with a rational approach to reality. Ironically enough, attacks on Macpherson in his own time did little to lessen the interest in, or the influence of, the poems.

Percy And The Ballads

Thomas Percy, a contemporary of Macpherson's, gave new stimulus to the interest in the Middle Ages by publishing three volumes of **ballads** from the early fifteenth century. These **ballads** were to serve as models for most of the English romantic poets-from Wordsworth and Coleridge to Keats and Shelley-who were looking for poetic forms which would be less restrictive than the heroic **couplet**, a form which had dominated eighteenth-century poetry. Coleridge, for instance, drew upon one of the **ballads** in this collection for the verse form of *The Rime of the Ancient Mariner*. The ballads, unlike Macpherson's Ossian poems, were genuine, although, like Macpherson, Percy altered them to accommodate the growing romantic taste.

The Gothic Tale Of Terror

The growing interest in medieval romance and the increasing emphasis on the imagination as opposed to reason produced in the last half of the eighteenth century the Gothic tale of terror. This forerunner of the modern detective mystery was characterized by a medieval setting and an ingenious plot. The author gave his imagination free reign, with sensational results, the narrative abounding in abductions, murders, and supernatural happenings.

Horace Walpole's *The Castle of Otranto* (1764) was the first novel to make full use of Gothic trappings. William Beckford's *Vathek* (1786), Ann Radcliffe's *The Mysteries of Udolpho* (1794), and Matthew Gregory Lewis' *The Monk* (1795) are the best and the most famous of the Gothic novels which flooded England during the second half of the century. The following passage from The Mysteries of Udolpho in which the heroine makes a frightful discovery is typical:

It may be remembered that in a chamber of Udolpho hung a black veil whose singular situation had excited Emily's curiosity and which afterward disclosed an object that had overwhelmed her with horror; for on lifting it, there appeared, instead of the picture she had expected, within a recess of the wall a human figure, of ghastly paleness, stretched at its length, and dressed in the habiliments of the grave. What added to the horror of the spectacle was that the face appeared partly decayed and disfigured by worms which were visible on the features and hands.

This attention to the horrifying aspects of death and decay anticipates nineteenth-century Gothic fiction such as Mary Shelley's *Frankenstein* and the tales of Edgar Allan Poe.

The Pre-Romantic Movement In Germany

Rousseau's romantic theories about man's nature and the nature of society helped inspire revolutions in American and France. In Germany, they caused no political revolution, but they found great favor with the young writers. Like their English and French counterparts, young German poets, dramatists, and novelists were beginning to rebel against the restraints of a rational age. It is to Rousseau and the translations of James Thomson's The Seasons, Macpherson's *Ossian* and Thomas Percy's *Reliques* that these German writers turned in their search for new poetic forms and modes of expression.

Sturm Und Drang

The youthful romantic spirit first made itself felt in German literature during the Sturm und Drang (storm and stress) period of the 1770s. As the name suggests, the period saw the rise of a literature informed by unrestrained emotion. Johann Gottfried von Herder, the father of the storm and stress movement, inspired a number of young writers, among them Goethe, to reject the values of neo-classicism for the new values of emotion and imagination. Herder, under the influence of Rousseau and the English pre-romantics, attacked neo-classic literature as coldly rational and imitative, praised Shakespeare for his natural genius and great imagination, and reawakened interest in national origins by publishing a group of German folk ballads. The storm-and-stress sensibility is exemplified by the lyric poetry of Friedrich Klopstock, Goethe's *The Sorrows of Young Werther* (1774), and Schiller's play *The Robbers* (1781). Klopstock celebrated love, nature, and freedom, while Goethe and Schiller dealt with the agonized frustrations of life and love.

The Flowering Of Romanticism

It is with the publication of Lyrical **Ballads** (1798), a joint poetic undertaking by Words-word and Coleridge, that romanticism began to flourish in England. The romantic spirit breathed new life into English poetry, and within a few years England saw the publication of Wordsworth's *Prelude*, Keats' *Odes*, Shelley's *Prometheus Unbound* and Byron's *Childe Harold*, *Manfred*, and *Don Juan*. A similar flowering occurred in Germany in 1797. The storm-and-stress movement and the efforts of Goethe and Schiller to marry romanticism to classicism in their later poetry facilitated the growth of romanticism, which became full-blown with the appearance of the poets Friedrich Holderlin (1770–1843) and Heinrich Heine (1797–1856), the dramatists Heinrich von Kleist (1777–1811) and Franz Grillparzer (1791–1872), and the novelist Jean Paul (1763–1825). Paradoxically, in France, which had given birth to Rousseau, one of the most influential romantic figures, romanticism did not develop further until the 1830s with the production of Victor Hugo's controversial play *Hernani*. Hugo, Lamartine (1790–1869), De Vigny (1797–1863), and Alfred De Musset (1810–1857) are the luminaries of French romantic poetry.

Essential Characteristics Of Romanticism

"You are only conscious of one impulse," Faust tells Wagner shortly after the play opens, "Never/Seek an acquaintance with the other. Two souls, alas, cohabit in my breast,/The one like a rough lover clings/To the world with the tentacles of its senses;/The other lifts itself to Elysian Fields/Out of the mist on powerful wings." This conflict, which tears Faust's soul, is common to all romantic writing. The romantic, like Faust, is pulled in two opposite directions: he desires to embrace the world of here-and-now, allowing his senses to respond fully to that world, and at the same time he longs to escape "on powerful wings" to a more perfect world. This transcendent world is generally informed by absolute beauty or love.

In English romantic poetry, the conflict was perhaps best exemplified in Keats. In *Ode on Melancholy* the poet recommends that the melancholy man "glut" his sorrow on "a morning rose," or on "the rainbow of a salt sand-wave," or on a "wealth of globed peonies." These objects of transient beauty would increase man's feeling of melancholy, thus making him more aware of himself and the world's beauty. In *Ode to a Nightingale*, the poet wishes to escape from this world "where men sit and hear each other groan" to the world of absolute beauty which the nightingale symbolizes: "Away! Away! for I will fly to thee,/Not charioted by Bacchus and his pards,/But on the viewless wings of Poesy."

Independence

The romantic often sees himself as an independent, wholly self-sufficient being. This feeling of independence prompts him to defy anyone, man or spirit, who would put himself on a higher plane. "Shall I yield to Thee, Thou shape of flame?" asks the defiant Faust in answer to the Earth Spirit's scorn of his puniness. "I am Faust, I can hold my own with Thee." Byron's Manfred, and in fact the Byronic hero as such, reacted to spiritual forces in a similar way. Shortly before his death at the end of the play, Manfred defies the spirit who summons him in words reminiscent of Faust: "Back to thy hell!/Thou never shalt possess me, that I know: What I have done is done; I bear within/A torture which could nothing gain from thine."

Love Of Death

Just before the Easter scene at the beginning of *Faust*, the protagonist contemplates suicide and in so doing suggests another characteristic of romantic literature: the love of death. "Be calm and take this step," says Faust at the end of a passage invoking death, "though you should fall/Beyond it into nothing-nothing at all." One sees a similar sentiment pervading nineteenth-century English and American romantic literature. "I have been half in love with easeful Death," wrote Keats in *Ode to a Nightingale*, "Called him soft names in many a mused rhyme,/To take into the air my quiet breath;/Now more than ever seems it rich to die."

In America, Poe argued that the death of a beautiful woman is the most poetic of all subjects, and in Whitman's *Out of the Cradle Endlessly Rocking*, death is the word whispered by the sea:

Whisper'd me through the night, and very plainly before daybreak, Lisp'd to me the low and delicious word death, And again death, death, death, death...

Like Faust and the speaker in Keats' *Ode*, Whitman was drawn to the idea of death; death is "delicious."

Emphasis On The Heart

Faust pronounces a romantic manifesto when he tells Wagner in lines 194–95, "But heart can never awaken a spark in heart/ Unless your own heart keep in touch." Faust's emphasis on the heart, thus on feeling, as opposed to the intellect, in man's dealings with his fellow man again makes him the archetypal romantic. This emphasis is found in romantic literature from Wordsworth to Whitman. "Come forth" said Wordsworth at the end of *The Tables Turned*, "And bring with you a heart/That watches and receives." It was also with the heart that Whitman responded in *Song of Myself*. "I loafe and invite the soul," said Whitman, following Rousseau's dictum to become an expansive spirit or heart, then exulting in his emotional response to life, "I see, dance, laugh, sing...."

And Rousseau foreshadowed them all when he said at the beginning of his *Confessions*, "Myself alone! I know the feelings of my heart, and I know men."

Love Of Humanity

One of the major distinctions between Faust and Wagner is that Faust embraces the humanity which Wagner scorns. In the Easter scene, Wagner no sooner declares that he is repelled by the vulgarity of the crowd than Faust accepts a drink from a member of the same crowd. At the end of the play, it is Faust's love of humanity which redeems him, a love which is made known in the opening lines of the play when he expresses a desire to improve mankind. This love of humanity is still another identifying characteristic of the romantic temperament. In *Lines Written in Early Spring* Wordsworth said that it grieved his heart "to think/What man has made of man." In *Hymn to Intellectual Beauty* Shelley considered the function of spiritual beauty and concluded with the declaration that beauty leads man to love of his fellow man: "Whom, Spirit fair, thy spells did bind? To fear himself, and love all humankind." Finally, it was this love which to a large degree informed Whitman's *Leaves of Grass*.

Love Of Nature

In order to escape from a world that was becoming ever more industrialized the romantic turned to nature. The return was inspired also by Rousseau when he argued that civilization corrupted man who was naturally good. If this is true, then the logical way of escaping corruption would be to return to nature. It is the Spring festival as well as the celebration of Easter which keeps Faust from suicide. It is nature which sustains man in Wordsworth's poetry. In *Tintern Abbey*, for instance, the poet exults in the pastoral scene and then relates how nature has sustained him in the city:

These beauteous forms Through a long absence, have not been to me As is a landscape to a blind man's eye: But oft, in lonely rooms, and 'mid the din Of towns and cities, I have owed to them In hours of weariness, sensations sweet, Felt in the blood and felt along the heart; And passing even into my purer mind, With tranquil restoration.

Alienation

Although romantics like Goethe, Wordsworth, and Shelley were led to embrace humanity, one also finds the romantic who has become alienated from the community, who has become the outsider. The Byronic hero exemplified this particular romantic characteristic. "Is it not better, then, to be alone," cries Byron's *Childe Harold* in Canto 71 of Childe Harold's Pilgrimage, "Is it not better thus our lives to wear,/Than join the crushing crowd, doomed to inflict or bear?" This **theme** of the hero as outsider is struck in the opening lines when Byron speaks of the **protagonist** as "The wandering outlaw of his own dark mind."

Spontaneity

One of the reasons that the medieval **ballads** attracted so much attention was that they attested to the value of spontaneous creation. Spontaneity and inspiration became the key words of romantic poetic theory. It was Shakespeare's spontaneous genius that was praised by Herder at the beginning of the Sturm und Drang period in Germany. And spontaneity was at the heart of Wordsworth's theory of poetry as formulated in the *Preface to the Lyrical Ballads*. "For all good poetry," asserted Wordsworth at the beginning of that essay, "is the spontaneous overflow of powerful feelings." Spontaneity as the heart of poetic creation was also pointed to by Shelley in *A Defense of Poetry* when he said, "A man cannot say, 'I will compose poetry.' The greatest poet even cannot say it; for the mind in creation is as a fading coal, which some invisible influence, like an inconstant wind awakens to transitory brightness; this power arises from within, like the color of a flower which fades and changes as it is developed, and the conscious portions of our natures are unprophetic either of its approach or its departure."

All of these elements influenced Goethe's work.

GENERAL SCHEME OF HIS WORK

Versatility

It is difficult indeed to assess the scope of a man as versatile as Johann Wolfgang von Goethe. He was an enormously prolific writer, and he worked steadily from his teenage years until just a few days before his death at the age of eighty-two. He excelled in many different types of literature, notably the drama, the **epic**, the novel, and the lyric poem; his autobiography is noteworthy; his literary criticism, if controversial, is nevertheless well worth reading. His diaries and letters have been collected, and are also of great interest. Obviously, his writing cannot be neatly categorized. That so much of it is still interesting, more than a century after his death, attests to its great power and to its universal significance.

Science

Goethe was not only a literary man, however. He also distinguished himself in scientific endeavors, contributing significant articles in the fields of botany, biology, and physics. These are generally considered to have been well ahead of their time and have made a significant contribution to the world of science. One must also consider his philosophical interests, which bridged his literary and scientific works; one can see in almost everything he wrote his relentless search for an absolute in which he could believe.

Social Figure

While Goethe was never an ordinary man, and was considered by many to be an eccentric, he nevertheless had a most distinguished political career. He served with distinction under Duke Charles Augustus, in Weimar, and held several posts of great importance. His significance in the world of current affairs can perhaps best be seen in his meeting with Napoleon; the Frenchman, who was certainly then the most significant political figure in Europe, paid tribute to Goethe as the most important literary figure of his time.

Obviously, then, Goethe was a man of renown. It is still not possible to come to any flat conclusion about his character, since his biographers and critics differ drastically in their evaluations of it. One can, however, make some dependable and valid generalizations about his writings.

Autobiographical Content

Before discussing the works, it should be said that nearly all Goethe's writing was at least in part autobiographical. This is one established fact on which all his critics agree, but it too has occasioned differences in interpretation. Some of his commentators have held that this autobiographical quality is a serious flaw in his work, limiting its general appeal. Others, however-perhaps most-hold that, whether autobiographical or not, his writing is among the greatest material to have been produced in the eighteenth and nineteenth centuries.

Kinds Of Writing

Drama

Goethe's first drama, published in 1773, was *Gotz von Berlichingen*. This play, which Goethe revised several times before its eventual appearance, was an instant success when it finally came out. Though it was set in the sixteenth century, it was an excellent statement of the **themes** of democracy and freedom for the common man, **themes** which are associated with the Romanticism of the late eighteenth and early nineteenth centuries.

Iphigenia At Tauris

This play, written in 1787, is an adaptation of the Greek play of the same name, written by Euripides. It too was an influential and popular work, but it is not marked by the same romantic spirit of "storm and stress" (Sturm und Drang) which characterized *Gotz*. Instead one finds here the spirit of the classical world which so impressed Goethe upon his trip to Italy. Iphigenia is marked by restraint, order, and simplicity, rather than by emotion.

Egmont

Egmont, like *Gotz*, has a historical and political **theme**. Published in 1787, it was popular on its appearance, but is not now considered to be as significant as his other dramas.

Torquato Tasso

This drama, which appeared in 1790, like *Iphigenia* shows the effects of Goethe's stay in Italy. It deals apparently with the life of Tasso, a major Italian poet, but the plot also recalls Goethe's own life and his trials as an artist in a political and social world.

Faust, A Tragedy

This poetic drama, upon which most of Goethe's fame now rests, occupied him during most of his writing lifetime. Although begun when he was a young man, in 1769, it was not finished until just before his death in 1832. At the age of 26, he had completed the Urfaust, an early version of the first part of the play. The manuscript of this work is a valuable supplement to the finished version; it presents many interesting points of comparison. In 1789 Goethe again took up work on the play, and in 1790 published *Faust: A Fragment*, a revision of the Urfaust. In 1800 he again started work on the drama, and wrote and revised it until his death.

The Historical Faust

The character on whom the play *Faust* is based actually lived in Germany in the late fifteenth and early sixteenth centuries. Reports indicate that he was a renowned practitioner of magic arts, and he is said to have revealed a pact made with the devil. In 1587 a book by Johann Spies recounted the semi-legendary life of Dr. Faust. The tale spread through Europe and was translated into English as *The History of the Damnable life and Deserved Death of Dr. John Faustus*. Christopher Marlowe, an English dramatist of Shakespeare's time, wrote a play in

1593 based on this book. It was called *The Tragical History of Doctor Faustus*, and is still considered one of the best plays in the English language.

Many other writers have used the life of Dr. Faust as a **theme** in plays, novels, and poems. One of the most recent is the novel *Doctor Faustus* (1948) by Thomas Mann.

Musical Treatments

Composers have also made use of the Faust **theme**. Among the musical works are *The Damnation of Faust* (1846) by Hector Berlioz, the opera *Faust* (1859) by Charles Gounod, and the opera *Mefistofeles* (1868) by Arrigo Boito.

Obviously, the story of Faust has been an inspiring one. Goethe's material was certainly not new, but what he did with it was significant. It is no mere tale of a man who made a bargain with the devil. Rather it is a universally meaningful story of man's attempts to gain knowledge, wisdom perfection, and of the eternal frustration of this striving. It has been criticized for lack of form and for some inconsistent characterization; most critics, however, agree that despite its admitted faults it ranks with the masterpieces of Shakespeare and Dante.

Novels

The Sorrows Of Young Werther: This novel, written in the form of letters, was printed in 1774. It is a somewhat sentimental and emotional story, dealing quite obviously with the lives of Goethe and his friends. It is also one of the best mirrors of the emotional turbulence of the Sturm und Drang period in literature. While it is perhaps too sentimental and romantic for the taste of the average twentieth-century reader, it received instant popularity and critical acclaim when it came out. It can still be profitably studied as one of the definitive statements of the young romantic writer.

Wilhelm Meister's *Apprenticeship* (1796) And Wilhelm Meister's *Travels*, Or *The Resigned* (1821-1829): These two companion novels again treat, quite obviously, Goethe's own life and trials, and his attempts to reflect meaningfully on them. The two books deal with a young man who tries to learn the ways of the world, becomes emotionally involved with many young women, and eventually reaps the rewards of a sober and dutiful life. They are not now considered to be of special value or significance, being loosely constructed and not very interesting, but they do represent Goethe's attempt to draw moral significance from his eventful life.

Other Poetry

Hermann Und Dorothea: Written in 1797, this work is classified by different critics as either a drama or an **epic** poem. Whatever its category, however, it remains immensely readable despite its great length. It is marked by classical restraint and interest in form, but its content is typically nineteenth-century; it expresses a romantic theory of love and glorifies the freedom of the individual.

Lyrics: Though Goethe is most remembered for his dramas, novels, and long poems, he also wrote a great many short lyrics. A survey of these shorter poems can be almost rewarding study for the student of Goethe, since in them one finds the progress from the passionate, "storm and stress" ridden young romantic to the more objective, tranquil, thoughtful, and philosophical old man. Many of these short poems have been set to music; among these is "The Erlking," a fanciful and thoroughly romantic **ballad** about a sick child who dies when threatened by elves. Some of his love poems are often found in volumes of continental literature; these include "The Heather-Rose," "Found," "Springtime All Year," "Wanderer's Night Song," and "Mignon."

Other Interests: Goethe's achievements in the field of literature, philosophy, and science are amazing indeed. He was also a gifted amateur in many other fields: he played several musical instruments, painted a great deal, enjoyed sports, and sometimes tried directing plays. He was also a formidable linguist; he knew seven languages and translated many major pieces of foreign literature into German. His collected works number well over one hundred volumes, far too many to be dealt with accurately in any one piece of criticism, but all rewarding to the student.

FAUST

INTRODUCTION

PREFACE

Much that is important in Goethe's tragedy has been discussed in the introduction or will be considered in the summary and supplementary sections that follow. However, the reader should bear in mind several additional questions during his reading.

The first question is: Is this a drama? When we read or see a play we expect certain things of it. Among them are continuity of **theme**, suspense, action, and dramatic interest. *Faust*, except in the portion of the first part concerned with the love affair between Faust and Gretchen, has none of these things. Although the first part is frequently performed on the stage, it is rarely performed in its entirety. And the second part is rarely performed at all. What, then, makes *Faust* a great play?

For one thing, a great deal is lost if we consider *Faust* only as a drama. Although it is written in dramatic form, it was not necessarily meant to be performed in its entirety. Goethe wrote *Faust* as a play because that was the form in which he could best present the story as he conceived it. But ultimately, *Faust* should be read as literature and not drama. The important things in the play are the ideas, and not the dramatic action.

The second question is similar: Is *Faust* a tragedy? Traditionally, a tragedy is concerned with a man's battle in the world to overcome his fate, his failure in this battle, and his death as a result. In *Faust*, all of the forces opposing the hero are supernatural ones and do not arrive because of anything he has done in life. It is true that he is a ready and willing subject for these forces, but in the last analysis he is merely a plaything of the gods and the devils. In addition, *Faust* has a happy ending. Faust dies, it is true, but he dies after living for 100 years. And he does not die lost and unhappy, but is instead on his way to heaven.

But in an important sense, *Faust* is a tragedy. It is the tragedy of a man always striving to reach for something more than he already has. It is the tragedy of a man who is never satisfied. In this way, the events in the play are a result of a typical human failing, and we can all understand Faust and sympathize with him as the drama unfolds.

Faust is an amazingly modern drama and Doctor Faust could be any one of us. Also, the play is structurally and thematically complex. The scenes shift back and forth from Heaven to earth, from the present to the past, and from reality to magic and witchcraft. However, we must be cautious about reading too much into these supernatural scenes. In his lifetime, Goethe himself ridiculed the critics who tried to point out the secret significance of the magic spells or formulas given in the play. And, to repeat, *Faust* is a drama of ideas. If we are to understand the actions of the play, we must be aware of the ideas that lie behind them.

It should be remarked that the play is written in verse, and not in prose. All the speeches are in **rhyme** and some of Goethe's greatest poetry is incorporated in this play. Often, the verse form is used for dramatic effect. Mephistopheles, for example, often mimics the people he is arguing with by speaking in the same meter and form that they do.

A note on translation: In the few instances where lines from the play are quoted in full, they are literal translations from the German and are not meant to reconstruct the meter or **rhyme** of the original.

THE DEDICATION

Dedication (lines 1-32)

In this short poem that precedes the dramatic scenes of *Faust*, we should imagine that the poet (Goethe) is sitting at his desk preparing to write his masterpiece.

He sees before his eyes the vague shapes that represent the characters and ideas he is trying to capture in his play. These shapes have haunted him since his youth, but now they swarm in his mind as never before. He recalls the days when the wavering forms first appeared to him, and he realizes that many of the people he knew then are gone. The shadows of friends and the women he loved, all dead now, appear to him as in a mist. None of the people who applauded his first efforts in poetry are around anymore to appreciate his greatest work; if they are not dead they have moved far away.

He becomes gripped by a resolution to put down on paper all the things he sees in his mind. He wants to bring into daylight those shadows from the past. His present life seems unimportant, and he feels that he must turn his attention to the sad reality of the past. He is ready to write the play.

Comment

The dedicatory poem actually represents Goethe's feelings when he began work on *Faust* again in 1797, after a lapse of almost ten years.

The forms or shadows referred to in the poem have a double meaning. They represent both the people Goethe knew in his youth and the ideas he wants to put into his play. This should give us a hint that Goethe's life and the action of Faust are interrelated. Many of the ideas of Dr. Faust are drawn from similar ideas that Goethe had at various periods in his life.

The poet's mood in the Dedication reveals much that is characteristic of Romanticism. The romantics were not concerned with the hard facts of life as it is lived here and now, but rather turned their attention to the emotions and yearnings that underlie life. One thing that interested them was recapturing the past, and recreating again all the tears and melancholy that examination of the past is likely to produce. As we have seen in the Dedication, this was Goethe's interest too.

THE PRELUDE

Prelude On The Stage (lines 33-242)

Like the Dedication, this brief scene has nothing to do with the dramatic action of *Faust*. However, it provides a skillful transition into the action that is to follow.

The scene is the stage of a theater. The three characters (the producer, the playwright, and a clown) are arguing about what makes a good play. The producer says that a good play is one that attracts big crowds to his theater. What the people want is surprise-they want to see something they have never seen before. And this, says the producer, is what the writer can give them.

The playwright replies that crowds do not interest him. If a poet writes only to fill a theatre, that poet will compromise his art. He writes for posterity, the playwright says, and not for the present.

The clown mocks the playwright and his talk of posterity. A good writer writes for the present, he says. But that does not mean he must compromise himself. He can write his own way and still please the people, by putting humor into the play.

It is the producer's turn again. He advises the playwright to fill his play with action, because that is what the people want. Don't be concerned with the unity of the plot, the producer says, just use any plot that has lots of room for action.

The playwright is insulted. He says that just because all the hacks write the way the producer wants does not mean that that should be a law of playwriting.

The manager says that the writer doesn't understand. People come to the theater after a hard day's work, and all they want is to be entertained. They do not come to be educated; they come merely because they are curious. Their thoughts are as much on getting drunk or meeting a girl after the play as on what's happening on stage.

If that's the way you feel, you had better look for another writer, the playwright retorts. For to construct a play that way would be to give up the poet's noblest right-that of making all the world see things the way he does. The writer's duty is to make each man realize the innermost accents of his being.

Comment

This is a romantic view of artistic creation. The writer is considered to be the only interpreter of life, the world itself is almost ignored.

To this the clown replies: Then live in this world, and not some other world of your own making. Conduct your art as if it were a love affair with life. Then everyone will come and listen to you.

I wish I were young again, the poet says. Everything seemed so simple then.

Youth is useful in war or in seducing young girls, the clown replies. But the artist needs the wisdom that comes with age, for an old man can reconcile the needs of youth with the realities of life.

The producer breaks into the dialogue. We have had enough talk, he says. Let's now produce a play. For while we are talking someone else is writing a successful play. Don't be so much concerned with ideals; instead, seize the possible. The stage has room for every kind of endeavor as long as it's interesting. Let us make a play that is interesting and dramatic, one that takes in all of Heaven and also includes Hell.

Comment

We are ready now to move on to the drama of *Faust*. The dialogue in the theater has shown three points of view about what a play is. The producer's views can be characterized as commercial: Anything, no matter how inartistic, that makes people want to come to his theater is good enough for him. The writers view is aesthetic: A good play is one written in accordance with the pure concepts of art, and the public be damned. The clown takes the practical approach. Art is fine, but the audience must also be taken into consideration. This good scene presents the idea that a play should combine these three points of view.

THE PROLOGUE

Prologue In Heaven (lines 243-353)

The action of *Faust* now begins. But it is a strange beginning, for it gives us a clue to what will happen at the very end of the play. It also presents the basic conflict of the drama, a conflict that should be kept in mind throughout all the adventures to follow.

The scene is set in Heaven. The Lord is seated on his throne, surrounded by his attendants, the angels. Mephistopheles, the Devil, is also a member of God's court and will become one of the principal characters in the play.

Comment

It is significant that the first scene takes place in Heaven. It shows us that what is to follow is out of the ordinary. We must expect the meaning of the play to apply not only to the characters it involves but to all the people on the earth.

The three archangels (Raphael, Gabriel, and Michael) step forward to declare the beauties of the universe. Raphael points out that the sun, although its movements are predetermined, is always a thing of wonder and beauty. Even the angels do not understand the mysteries of the universe, he says, but their lack of knowledge gives them strength, for they realize they are in the presence of something unfathomably perfect. Every time the sun rises, Raphael says, the world appears as glorious as it did on the first day.

Gabriel's poem is about the earth. As the earth speeds on its course around the sun and spins on its axis there is constant change, he says. Day succeeds night and the ocean tides shift back and forth on the rocks of the shore. Michael tells of the great power that is in the universe, giving as examples tempests and thunder. And yet the Lord can control these forces, he says, adding that the angels admire the still and mild days that He produces in the midst of all the power and violence.

The three archangels then join together to repeat in chorus the assertions made in Raphael's speech. All the great creations of the Lord are as glorious as on the day they were made, the angels conclude.

Comment

The angel's view of the universe is an important one. What they are saying, in effect, is that a man on earth should never be bored. For, although the days of his life might seem to be monotonously the same, man would never be unhappy if he realized that the universe is so great and so perfect that it can never repeat itself. Rather than be bored or attempt to investigate the mysteries of life, man should have nothing but admiration for what the Lord was quoted. This view is important because of Faust and Mephistopheles oppose it. They believe that man is doomed to be unhappy and that the reason for his unhappiness is the intelligence God has given him. One of the most significant outcomes of the play will be the shifting of Faust's ideas from agreement with Mephistopheles to agreement with the angels.

Mephistopheles steps forward from the crowd of the Lord's attendants. He expresses happiness at once again being near the Lord and says he is the Lord's humble servant.

Comment

We may be surprised to find Mephistopheles, the Devil, in Heaven with all the angels. However, according to Christian theology, the devils were once angels who fell from God's grace when they tempted Adam and Eve in the Garden of Eden. This is where the expression "fallen angels," meaning devils, comes from. There is also a Biblical precedent for having the Devil confer with God. In the Old Testament Book of Job, the Lord allows Satan to tempt Job, a holy man, and Satan tries to make Job renounce the Lord. In fact, the story of Job closely parallels in several respects the story of Faust. The presence of Mephistopheles in Heaven can also be interpreted as showing that the presence of evil (in the form of the Devil) is necessary to bring out the goodness of man.

Mephistopheles continues. He cannot match the angel's eloquent speeches, he says slyly. If he tried, he would only make the Lord laugh, except that the Lord never laughs. He cannot praise the sun or the earth, the Devil declares. All he has noticed is that men on earth are unhappy. And the reason for their unhappiness is "the gleam of heavenly light"-intelligence-that God has given them, he says. Reason, or intelligence, causes men's lives to be even worse than the lives of animals, Mephistopheles asserts. Mephistopheles compares man's activities to those of the grasshopper, who jumps around and flies through the air because he is never satisfied just to sit in the grass. But all the jumping around never does him any good because when he finally comes back to the grass he finds that nothing has changed. And every bit of dung man sees he wants to stick his nose in, the Devil concludes.

Comment

There are several points we should note about Mephistopheles' first speech. Most important, we see right away that he has a sharp mind and a clever tongue. Many of the Faust plays before Goethe's made the Devil a bumbling dolt who was no match for God or the principles of goodness. But Goethe's Mephistopheles is supremely intelligent and witty, and he is a worthy opponent for the Lord. He makes God appear foolish in his speech:

My pathos would surely make you chuckle, If you had not forgotten how to laugh.

The accusation that the Lord lacks a sense of humor is perfect, because it is true. The remark punctures the solemnity of the gathering in Heaven, and brings us down to basic things. We will see this happen often in the play. Time and time again, Mephistopheles will destroy people's sentimental ideas with his sharp use of reason and wit. Many commentators have called Mephistopheles one of the great examples of rational man in action.

Another thing we immediately learn about Mephistopheles is his view of man. We remember that the archangels said that the universe was perfect, even if they didn't understand how it worked. The Devil disputes this view. The universe is not perfect, he says, because man is unhappy in it. And the reason for his unhappiness is his intelligence. Man is even worse off than the animals, for at least the animals know their place and do not run around looking for answers. But poor unhappy man is always sticking his nose into things that should not concern him. This opposition of views between the Devil and the angels is the great **theme** of *Faust*.

The Lord replies to Mephistopheles' first speech. "Can't you do anything but abuse?" He asks. "Don't you find anything on earth that is right?"

Things on earth are as bad as they can be, Mephistopheles retorts. I don't even have the heart to use my evil influence on man, the Devil says, because man is in enough trouble as it is.

Now the Lord asks a crucial question: "Do you know Faust?"

Mephistopheles is surprised. "You mean the doctor?" he says.

"That's the one, God replies. "My servant."

Comment

This is our introduction to the character for whom the play is named. We realize that he is not an ordinary man, for both God and the Devil have been keeping their eyes on him. The chain of events has begun that will involve Dr. Heinrich Faust for the rest of his life.

You call Faust your servant, Mephistopheles says, but he is certainly serving you in strange ways. He is trying to communicate with spirits because he is not satisfied with ordinary things. He wants to experience all the joys of life, and even that would not be enough for him. And worst of all, he almost knows how foolish his attempts are.

He is confused now, the Lord replies, but soon I will lead him to better things. He is like a young tree that has not yet come into bloom.

What will you bet? Mephistopheles asks. If you let me do what I want with him, I can turn him away from God and capture his soul for the Devil.

The Lord agrees to wager. As long as Faust is alive the Devil may try to influence him, He says. For as long as a man is alive he will fall into error.

Good, Mephistopheles says. For I would much rather work on someone who is alive than on a corpse.

You are free to try with Faust, the Lord retorts. But in the end you will have to admit that a good man always remembers the right road, even though he strives for unholy things.

We shall see, says Mephistopheles. When I win I hope you will not go back on the bet, he says to the Lord. For under my guidance Faust will learn to eat dust like my relative, the snake.

I won't go back on the bet, the Lord says. For I don't hate the devils. Of all the forces of evil in the world the ones who are active and witty give me the least trouble. The real danger for man comes if he just sits and does nothing. It will be good for Faust to have an evil companion to keep him busy, the Lord concludes. Then God returns to address the angels. You are my sons, he says. Sing the praises of love and beauty and rejoice in everything that works and lives. Give the permanence and perfection of Heaven to the impermanence and imperfection of life.

The heavens close and the archangels go their ways. Mephistopheles is left alone.

I get a kick out of seeing the Old Boy now and then, the Devil says. I try to be nice to him because it's interesting to see the Lord conversing politely with the Devil.

Comment

Thus the famous bet between God and the Devil is made. The stake is the soul of Faust; whoever has gained control of him at the time of his death will get his immortal soul. It may seem that Faust himself is just a pawn in the game between the Lord and Mephistopheles. But we will soon see that he has a mind and voice of his own, and will have a great deal to say about the outcome of the play. The Lord, who we must remember is all-powerful, has said that he will prevail in the end, so we have a hint as to how the play will conclude. But Mephistopheles is so clever that we will not know for sure until the last line. We are now ready to go on to the First Part of the Tragedy of *Faust*.

FAUST

TEXTUAL ANALYSIS

PART ONE

PART I

Night (lines 354–807)

As the curtains part, we find Dr. Heinrich Faust alone in his study. The room is narrow, with a high ceiling, and is cluttered with books and scientific instruments. The time is the sixteenth century; the place is a large city in Germany. Dr. Faust is a middle-aged man. He is one of the most famous doctors and scholars of his day. He is sitting at his desk, restless and bored with his studies. He launches into a long monologue expressing his present state of mind.

Dr. Faust is close to despair. He has studied philosophy, law, medicine, and theology through and through, he says, and still finds himself no wiser than when he began. He has a master's degree and a doctorate and for ten years has been a teacher. Even when he is teaching, he realizes he knows nothing. He has not hesitated to investigate everything that interested him, no matter what the authorities or the Church said about it. "I am not afraid of the Devil or Hell," Faust says. But he finds no joy in learning, and has not discovered anything that would better the lot of man. He has neither money nor worldly honors; it is a dog's life, he says.

Comment

We should note immediately the desperation in Faust's voice. He is ready to try anything. His problem, we see already, is that he wants to obtain some significant knowledge. He wants to find out what holds the universe together, or what can make man really happy. Most of all, he wants delight and joy in his work and in his life.

Faust continues his monologue. So I have studied magic too in order to see if that can solve any of the mysteries of life, he says. I wish I didn't have to keep on saying that I don't know, the doctor continues. I wish I could see the secret force that rules the world and determines its course. I wish I could create something, instead of repeating phrases out of books.

The doctor addresses himself to the moon shining through his window. I wish this were the last time you had to shine on my despair, he says. How often have I looked up from my papers and dusty books and seen you. I wish I could float with spirits in the sky near you, he says. I wish I could give up all this studying and just live under the moon. Then he returns to earth, and looks around his study. I'm still a mole in this dark dungeon, he says. My only company is my books, and they are dusty and worm-eaten. The only thing my chemicals and instruments and broken-down furniture are good for is to collect more dust. This is my world, he says, and a very poor world it is. God made man to experience nature in all its freshness and purity. And instead my existence is confined to this musty chamber that reeks of death. Is it any wonder I am anguished?

Faust turns his attention to his magic, so that he can escape from his dusty boredom. He picks up a book written by Nostradamus, the famous French alchemist and magician of the Middle Ages. Magic will free my soul, the doctor says, and show me the stars in orbit. I could study these magic symbols and give a rational explanation of them, he says. But I am tired of study; I want to experience the symbols, to feel them in my own body.

Faust opens the book to a symbol of the universe. He studies it. Suddenly his mood changes. I feel a young and holy joy at this sight, he says. I feel jubilation in every nerve. I feel all the mystery of nature around me, as if I could almost touch it.

Comment

In this scene we see one of the outstanding characteristics of Faust-his constant striving for something beyond the ordinary. We found him in boredom and despair. But suddenly, when his mind turns to magic and spirits, he becomes full of joy. This will happen time and again in the play. Faust will progress further and further into the world of spirits, but he will never be satisfied. He will always want to see what is around the next corner or over the next mountain. He constantly overextends himself. When he falls in love, he will want his love to be deeper than any ever known before. When he becomes rich and powerful, he will want even more power and wealth. This trait of character, this constant striving for something bigger and better, has been given a name by critics of Western culture-"Faustian." The Faustian personality is one that is always reaching out for the ultimate, the infinite, the perfect, the absolute.

Faust returns his gaze to the symbol in the book. "Am I a god?" he asks. This page seems to glow with light. I can believe that old saying: If you open up your mind and your heart, you will find a world of spirits not far away from the world you have known before.

The universe symbol fascinates Faust. It seems to draw all the fragmentary aspects of life together and to unify them. Through the power of the symbol the world appears to him like a giant ferris wheel. The compartments on the wheel dip down to earth and then ascend to Heaven; then the process is repeated.

Then a change comes over the doctor. He realizes his joy is only an illusion, like a play on the stage. The symbol produces deep emotions in him, but when he tries to analyze his emotions with his intellect the whole thing falls apart. It is like a circle: there is no beginning and no end. He cannot find the point on the circle at which to say: "This is where it all begins." There is no place where he can find the source of nature. And so, realizing the impossibility of his quest, Faust returns (but only for a moment) to the despair in which we found him when the scene began.

Comment

We have learned another important aspect of the character of Dr. Heinrich Faust. His temperament is constantly changing. One moment we will find him on the heights of bliss, and the next moment in the depths of despair. The reason for the change this time is one we will meet again and again in the scenes to follow: he has been carried away by vague emotions and is disappointed when he examines these emotions and finds that they get him no closer to his goal (finding out the secrets of the universe). Remember what Mephistopheles said in the Prologue in Heaven: Man is unhappy because he has intellect. Here we find a good example of his contention. Faust was inexpressibly happy until he examined his joy rationally and found that it was nothing.

Dr. Faust turns to another symbol in the book of magic. This time it is a symbol representing the earth. I feel a closer kinship to this symbol, he says. I look at it and I feel I can conquer any of the forces on earth. Whereas the symbol of the universe led me to things too vast and complex to understand, the symbol of the earth leads me to things I think I know. I could be happy within the confines of the earth, if only my mind did not lead me to Heaven and spirits that are outside the world.

Suddenly a change comes over Faust's narrow and dusty room. Through the window, he sees a dark cloud pass between him and the moon. The lamp on his desk flickers. He feels the presence of a spirit near him and declares himself ready to give his body up to it, even if it costs him his life.

He grabs the magic book and pronounces the secret words that will make the spirit visible. A flash of red flame runs through the room, and then the spirit steps out of the flame.

Comment

At first, all of this talk about spirits and magic might seem impossible at best and silly at worst. But from the beginning this was not a realistic play. The Prelude on the Stage was about abstract concepts of art, although real people were involved in the discussion of the concepts. And the play actually began with the Prologue in Heaven. Heaven, we should remember, is a supernatural place, just as God and his angels and Mephistopheles are supernatural beings. After leaving Heaven we have been taken by Goethe to a real place on earth-Dr. Faust's study. But no sooner are we in the study and barely acquainted with the doctor than the talk of spirits and magic begins. This will happen throughout the play. There are many scenes that could only take place on the earth with real people, notably the sensual love affair that we shall encounter shortly. Here will be shown seduction and murder, things that could only happen on earth. But the **theme** of the play is something that cannot be brought out by using merely people and their earthly emotions. For the **theme** involves a man's struggle to go beyond the world to a consideration of the universe as a whole. Goethe has chosen to present this **theme** through the medium of spirits and by skillful transitions from the real world to the spirit world and back again. The spirits are, of course, not to be taken at face value; they represent things that are going on in Faust's mind.

The spirit that Faust has summoned speaks. "Who calls me?" it asks. Faust turns away from it in terror. "I cannot bear to look at you," he says.

You have asked for me to come, the spirit says, and now all you can do is turn away. Just a moment ago you were saying you would risk death to get close to me, and now all you do is shiver. You talked of your courage to face any of the forces of the world, as if you were a superman. You talked of your great joy at being close to the spirits. And now you turn out to be a miserable, frightened worm.

I will not run, Faust retorts. I am as good as you are. I am Faust.

The spirit describes its life. I wander to and fro over the world, it says, and experience constant change. Birth and death, war and peace-all these I have known. My duty is to weave the garment that God makes men wear.

If you wander through the universe, then I am close to you, Faust says.

You may think that you are close to me, the spirit replies. But you are in reality only close to the image of me that you have formed in your mind. With this, the spirit disappears.

Faust collapses in despair. He doesn't understand. I thought that God made man in His own image, he says. And yet I am not even like that spirit.

Comment

Here is revealed the tragic flaw in the character of Dr. Faust, the flaw that will endanger his soul throughout the play. It is, very simply, that Faust has chosen to try to be like God. He has remembered this statement from his reading of the Book of Genesis in the Bible: "And God said, let us make man in our image, after our likeness: and let him have dominion over the fish of the sea, and over the fowl of the air, and over the cattle, and overall the earth, and over every creeping thing that creepeth on the earth. So God created man in His own image, in the image of God created Him." But this Biblical quotation describing how God created man mentions only man's material life on earth. It does not say anything of man's mind, nor does it give man instruction on how he is to use his intellect. However, Faust has assumed that if God created man in His own image, then man is entitled to use his reason to emulate the intellect of God.

According to the statements of the angels, man's duty is not to create, as God does, but merely to live in wonder of God's power. Faust does not subscribe to these statements. He believes that a thinking man should analyze life and then go beyond it to question the sources of life. He believes that if man learns the secrets of the universe he can exercise the same power that God does. This is Faust's error. He does not have the humility to know that God is greater than he is. But he will learn it. As God said in the Prologue in Heaven: "Faust is My servant."

There is a knock at the door to Faust's room. He realizes that it is his famulus (assistant), Wagner. He silently berates the assistant for disturbing his visions.

Wagner, dressed in a nightgown and a sleeping cap, enters with a lantern in his hand. Faust turns away from him in disgust.

Excuse me, Wagner says. I heard you talking and I thought you were reading aloud from some Greek tragedy. I would like to learn the art of dramatic reading, for I have heard that it is useful.

Comment

In the play, Wagner is a figure of fun. He is not very bright and will frequently be used to provide comic relief from the deep and serious thoughts of Faust. Here, for example, he intrudes on one of the most important moments in Faust's life and asks his teacher for a lesson in public speaking. But beyond the obvious comic characteristics of Wagner there is something else that is close to the **theme** of the play. That "something else" is Wagner's desire, like Faust's, to know everything. But if we examine the difference between what Wagner means by knowing everything and what Faust means by the same statement, we will discover what an extraordinary man Faust is. All Wagner wants, in his simplistic and mechanical way, is to be exposed to all the knowledge there is in the world. He is like a student; who believes that if he memorizes the *Encyclopedia Britannica* he will become a wise man. The truth of the matter is, of course, that all the knowledge in the world is no good to a man unless he applies it to his own life. Wagner thinks that knowledge is an end in itself. Faust has gone beyond this view; he realizes that if learning is to do him any good it must serve only as a key to the understanding of the universe and man's place in it. Faust has found out through bitter experience that knowledge in itself cannot make a man happy. At this point in the play he thinks that magic might release him from his dilemma. He will find out later that a deeper kind of religion is the answer. Thus, in the scenes that follow, it is useful to compare what Wagner has to say about learning with what Faust has to say about the same subject.

Wagner continues his discussion of public speaking. Since I spend most of my time studying, Wagner says, and rarely go out into the world, how can I control it from such a distance with only the fine use of words?

If you do not feel in your heart what you say with your voice, any attempt at persuasion is useless, Faust replies. No matter how much you read about speaking, no matter how much you practice dramatic reading, it will not do any good when you use it unless the words come from the depths of your soul. Children and monkeys might be impressed by fancy talk, but you will never create anything meaningful unless you believe what you say.

Simple Wagner does not understand. Doesn't a lot depend on how you say something? he asks.

Don't be a noisy fool, Faust retorts. Don't look for the easy way out. If something makes sense, you can explain it to the world without using fancy tricks of public speaking. A fancy speech is like a foggy wind rustling the dead leaves on a tree.

Wagner takes refuge from Faust's attack by mouthing a sentimental speech that demonstrates the very thing Faust is talking about. Oh God, art is long and life is short, Wagner says foolishly. We scholars spend all our wretched energy on reading and studying, and just as we get near the source of knowledge we find that we are dead.

Do you really think the source of knowledge is in books? Faust asks. I tell you again, if you do not find the source of knowledge within yourself, then you will never find it.

Excuse me, Wagner says. But it seems so wonderful to participate in history by reading what the wise men before us believed. It seems to me that we are only continuing their work, and eventually we will achieve the height of knowledge.

To achieve the height of knowledge is not like climbing a ladder, Faust replies. For we cannot truly know what the people before us were thinking. What we get from their books is only a pale reflection of their times. It is like examining a dust bin or a storage attic. At best it is like seeing a puppet play.

This is too much for me, Wagner says in despair. I thought everyone, by studying the past, could get a glimpse of what the world really means.

How misguided you are! Faust replies. Only a few men in history have been able to see beyond the illusions of the world and to grasp the ultimate realities. And these few, joyful in the knowledge they had gained, proclaimed their discoveries to the common people. And what they discovered was too much for the people to stand. All these adventures into the unknown were burned or crucified by the people they hoped to enlighten.

Comment

The scene we have just read is of crucial importance to the understanding of the play and to a fuller realization of what the complex Dr. Faust is really after. The best approach to the scene is through consideration of the time it is supposed to represent. Remember, Faust is a man of the sixteenth century. Although many of the ideas in the play could just as well apply to our own time and our own minds, the real setting for the drama is Germany in the period 1520–1540. (Indeed, this is one of the tests of a great work of art. It must of course be concerned with a specific time and place, but in the end it must also apply to all times and all places.) So, to understand Faust more fully, we must consider what was going on in Germany in the beginning of the sixteenth century. First of all, it was a time when the full force of the Renaissance was being felt in Germany. The Renaissance began in Italy in the fourteenth century, and from there it spread to the rest of Europe in the next three hundred years. The basic conception of the Renaissance was a simple one, although its effects were far from simple. That conception was that the center of the universe was not God, or the sun, or nature, or Aristotle-but man himself. In the Middle Ages, individual man was considered to be insignificant. The weight of knowledge accumulated through the ages-notably the system of Aristotle, the Greek philosopher, and the adaptation of Aristotle by St. Thomas Aquinas, the great spokesman for the ruling Catholic Church-was considered more important than anything an individual human being could contribute to it. Thus, man in the Middle Ages was confined within a system of belief, controlled by the Catholic Church, that he had no way of affecting. (Note how similar Wagner's view is to the general view of medieval man.) Then came the Renaissance. The great thinkers of this great period freed man from his medieval prison. Man was proclaimed to be the beginning and the end of all endeavor on the earth. Nothing that was not useful to man's life in the world was kept in the Renaissance intellectual system. This system, known as Humanism (after the human being to whom it was directed), cleared the medieval cobwebs out of men's minds.

In Germany, this change took hold later than it did in Italy. The outstanding effect of the Renaissance on Germany was the Protestant Reformation of Martin Luther. Luther, dissatisfied with the prevailing stuffy theology and practices of the Church of Rome, proclaimed in 1517 a new Christian system. (Remember that Faust lived during the same time that Luther did.) Luther's main thesis was that man himself could interpret the meaning of the Christian religion and did not need an all-powerful church to do it for him. He thus applied the main teaching of the Renaissance-man's self-sufficiency-to his own society and his own church. This, then, is where we find Dr. Faust.

When Faust said to Wagner: "To achieve the heights of knowledge is not like climbing a ladder," he meant that this is the Renaissance and not the Middle Ages. Wagner thinks that if you pile all the books you have read on top of each other you will be able to climb on top of them and reach the heights of knowledge. Faust, being a man of the Renaissance, knows that this is not true. Man cannot understand fully what those before him have thought, he says. If we go back to the Middle Ages, when most of our books were written, it will be like going back to an attic filled with useless things, he says. It will be like seeing a puppet show in which we are the puppets and the writers of the Middle Ages are the ones who are putting the words into our mouths. Instead of looking back into the past, Faust believes that he must look into the depths of his own being for the knowledge that he so passionately seeks. Faust is truly a man of the Renaissance. He believes he is capable of achieving anything he wants by using his own capabilities. He does not need the crutch provided by the writers of the past. Faust has not yet achieved his full capabilities. He has some way to go before he realizes that he cannot find the whole way by himself- he must learn still that the tender mercies of the universe will not go in his favor unless he gives himself up to them. But we must know too that those tender mercies can be found within man himself.

But enough of this talk, Faust says to Wagner. It is very late and we must break off this session.

I enjoyed our intellectual conversation, and would have liked to stay awake longer, Wagner says. But tomorrow is Easter Sunday; maybe we can talk again then. In parting, Wagner delivers himself of another simple, sentimental statement: "I have pursued my studies with diligence and I know quite a bit, but I would like to know everything.

Faust is left alone. He thinks what a fool Wagner is, and yet is thankful that he broke into his session with the spirit. If Wagner had not come, I might have lost my senses, says Faust. For when the spirit said I was not equal to the gods, it disturbed me deeply. It was a great shock to find that I have to exist as a human after all. But that is the way of the world. No matter how happy our illusions make us, sooner or later they come crashing down. I am not like the gods; I am a beast like all the rest.

Faust looks round his study. Those books will do me no good, he says. Nor those instruments I once thought would reveal to me the secrets of nature. It would have been better if I had spent my money on liquor or girls; for I have all these book and tools and potions and what have they brought me? Happiness? No. Knowledge? No. Nothing.

The doctor's gaze is attracted to a dark corner of his study. Why do I keep looking at that corner? he asks himself. What is that bottle that seems to shine so brightly there? Faust goes over and takes it down from the shelf. It is a distillation of sleeping drugs and fatal powders. It is a poison Faust has brewed himself. It will give him a painless death.

Comment

We found Faust in deep despair. Through two long monologues he has revealed his state of mind to us. The conversation with Wagner provided an interlude between the monologues. Now we have come to the logical conclusion of Faust's depression: attempted suicide.

Faust resolves to take the poison to get relief from all his worldly pain and boredom. When I take this potion it will prove that I am like the gods, Faust says, for they are not afraid of death and neither am I.

To drink his poison, Faust takes from its case an old crystal goblet that belonged to his father. Faust remembers that his father used it to serve liquors at his banquets. The guests would take a drink and then look into the goblet and tell in verse the visions they saw there. Faust says ironically that he will have no time for poetry once he takes a drink from the goblet now. The doctor raises the glass high: "With all my soul I offer this last drink as a salute to the morning," he says.

Suddenly, just as Faust is about to down the potion, the dawn breaks. The Easter bells in the town begin their joyous peal and a choir of angels sings: "Christ is risen."

Faust takes the goblet from his lips in astonishment. Is it Easter? he asks. Is this the song that was sung around Christ's tomb when he arose from the dead?

Comment

Faust is saved from suicide. It is interesting to note that his salvation comes just at dawn. We remember that the archangel Raphael said that every morning the world is made new and as glorious as on the first day. We will find several times in the play that Faust is refreshed and saved from further trouble by the dawn.

A choir of women takes up the Easter hymn. They recall that the women of Jerusalem mourned Christ's crucifixion and then dressed his body in linen and put it in the tomb. "Christ is risen," the chorus of angels repeats.

Why should this Easter ritual affect me? Faust asks. Although I hear the words, I do not believe. And yet somehow the music calls me back to life. I recall all the tender thoughts of my youth. Now that memory brings me back from death's doorway. The earth has reclaimed me.

The choir of angels sings again: "Christ is risen." Jesus is near to everyone, the angels sing. (The scene closes.)

Before The City Gate (lines 808-1177)

It is the afternoon of Easter Sunday. A holiday throng is passing through the gates of the city to spend the day out in the country. All of the young men discuss the best places to pick up girls and various suggestions are made. The girls, too, talk among themselves about the best places to find boys. Apprentices, soldiers, servant girls, and citizens of the town are all looking for company of the opposite sex. They talk of things that people everywhere talk of: girls, boys, taxes, wars, and having a good time.

Faust and Wagner join the crowd. Faust talks about spring. The sun is melting the snow and freeing the ice in the rivers and streams, he says. Nature is taking on the colors of summer; but for the moment most of the color is provided by the clothes of the holiday throng. The people have emerged into the sunshine after a long winter indoors. They are happy. Here, with them, I can feel human and enjoy my humanity.

It is a great honor to take a walk with you, Wagner says. But I myself could never make the mistake of taking pleasure in the doings of the common people.

Under a linden tree, a group of peasants are dancing and singing. They sing a merry song of love and seduction.

An old peasant approaches Faust. It is good of you to come out among us, he says. You are a great scholar and we find you among us. Have a drink. Faust accepts and proposes a toast to the crowd's health. The peasants gather around him. The old peasant recalls that Faust's father saved many of their lives during a plague. And Faust himself, though a young man then, tirelessly helped his father, the peasant says. All of the peasants toast Faust as a man who has helped them greatly.

Comment

This is an aspect of Faust's character that we must not forget. He is a great physician and has done much to help the people. He is not a musty scholar who has made no attempt to live outside his study. He has been through the world and wants something beyond it.

Faust advises the peasants to pray to God, Who always sends help. Then he and Wagner go on their way.

It must be a great thing to have everyone know you and pay homage to you, Wagner says to Faust.

Faust makes a cynical answer. My father and I killed as many people as we helped with our crude medicines, he says. It is very ironic that now I hear myself praised for all my mistakes.

You should not be unhappy over that, Wagner says. Your father gained a certain amount of knowledge and passed it on to you. Now you in turn can add to your father's knowledge and reach still higher.

It must be wonderful for someone like you, Faust says caustically. You still hope to rise out of the sea of errors that is the world. The fact of the matter is, says Faust, that the things one knows are of no use. What is important are the things you do not know. But let's not talk about unpleasant things. Look how the sun is setting over the town. I wish I had wings to soar over the world and follow the sun on its course. But man is the wingless animal, although it is his lot always to wish for wings.

I am a bit of an eccentric myself, says Wagner in his usual stupid manner, but I have never wished for wings. One soon gets sick of nature. What I like is books, which feed my spiritual being. To me, turning page after page of a book is like flying.

You are lucky, Faust says. You are only uneasy because you cannot read enough books to satisfy you. I am uneasy for two reasons, and one is warring against the other. One part of me clings to the earth while the other aspires to the skies.

> Comment

These few lines of verse are crucial to an understanding of *Faust*. They are so famous and so important that they bear repeating in full.

Alas, two souls are living in my breast, And one wants to separate itself from the other. One holds fast to the world with earthy passion And clings with twining tendrils: The other lifts itself with forceful craving To the very roof of heaven.

This is a perfect expression of Faust's "split personality." One part of him is bound to the earth and all its pleasures; the other part wants to leave the earth and mingle with the stars. It also reveals his romantic spirit.

Faust says that if he could get in contact with the spirits and soar to the stars, he would forsake all his earthly longings.

Do not invoke the terrible spirits, Wagner says. They may seem to bring benefits, but actually hidden under their pleasant exterior is a cesspool of evil. They cannot be trusted. But it's getting cool, Wagner says. Let's go home. Then Wagner looks over at Faust and asks, What are you staring at?

Do you see that black dog running around there? Faust asks. What do you think he is?

Just a lost dog, Wagner replies.

It is circling around us, Faust says. And it is leaving a trail of sparks.

I see the poodle, but I don't see any sparks, Wagner says.

It seems to me he is trying to cast a magic spell on us, Faust says.

Nonsense, Wagner retorts. He is just a friendly dog. Look how he wags his tail.

Come here and walk with us, Faust says to the black poodle.

You see, says Wagner, it's just a well-trained dog who knows a lot of tricks. I guess you're right, Faust says.

The two scholars pass through the gate to the city, on their way home.

PART 2

Faust's Study (lines 1178–1529)

Faust enters the room with the poodle he has found during his day's outing. It is night again. It has been a great day, Faust says. I have learned to honor the life of man and I am almost ready to succumb to the love of God.

The black poodle growls and jumps around the room at these words. Faust commands the dog to be quiet and continues his meditations.

I am hopeful that I can conquer my despair, Faust says. Perhaps I can arrive at a reasonable solution to my dilemma and become satisfied with my earthly life.

The poodle snarls again. Be quiet, Faust commands. I have seen many men snarl at things they do not understand; perhaps dogs do the same thing.

Then a change comes over Faust. He is no longer hopeful or content with his lot. I must turn again to the supernatural, Faust says, and he takes up a copy of the New Testament and begins to read. He is going to try to translate it into German.

"In the beginning was the word," Faust reads. Then he debates with himself whether the keyword should be "word," "mind," or "act." The poodle continues his antics. Faust orders him from the room. But the poodle does not go, and instead begins to change shape. Faust is at first surprised, and then decides to use magic to make the dog take the shape of whatever is inside it.

Faust recites a series of magic spells while a chorus of spirits chants in the corridor. The dog takes on various shapes; It becomes like a hippopotamus with flashing eyes, then like an elephant. Some of Faust's spells do not affect the creature, but finally the doctor finds the right one and the room begins to quake. The dog disappears behind the stove as Faust threatens to use the full power of his magic. A mist surrounds the stove.

From behind the stove steps Mephistopheles, dressed as a traveling scholar.

Comment

Thus we meet the Devil again. We shall not lose sight of him for long throughout the rest of the tragedy. This is also the turning point in Faust's life. So far we have learned a great deal about the doctor's character and his mood. Now we shall see Mephistopheles lead this man, whom we have come to know, through the depths and heights of existence.

Faust is astounded when Mephistopheles appears. Is this all that was inside the poodle, a traveling scholar? he asks in amusement.

Congratulations on your use of magic Mephistopheles says. You really made me sweat.

Who are you? Faust asks.

That's a silly question for a man like you, the Devil says. For my name is only an outward appearance of my real being, and you have shown that you value reality above all else.

Sometimes a lot is revealed in a name, Faust says. But enough of the talk. Who are you?

I am a part of that force that always wants evil and yet creates good, Mephistopheles replies. I am the spirit that negates. Sin, destruction, and evil are the things I prize.

You call yourself only a part of the evil force, Faust asserts. And yet you are a whole person as you stand before me.

Comment

Only Faust could ask this question. With his extreme belief in the capacities of individual man and his constant striving to make use of all the capacities he thinks he has, Faust cannot understand a man (or a devil) who admits that he is only a part of the total scheme of things. As we have seen, one of the things Faust will learn is that a man cannot do and be everything. Every man, if he is to be happy, must learn his place in the world and in the universe. This applies as much to a great scholar and doctor as it does to the poorest peasant. Actually, Mephistopheles' answer to Faust's question (given below) does not indicate the Devil's position. Mephistopheles is being sly and modest to gain the doctor's confidence, for Mephistopheles too believes that in order to be happy a man must have everything he wants. This belief is the basis of the bargain that Faust makes with Mephistopheles in the next scene.

Only man is foolish enough to think that because he is a single person he must be whole and complete, Mephistopheles replies. I realize that I am only a part of the darkness that once covered the world. That darkness gave birth to light, and now the two are in constant battle for control of the universe. But the light always loses because it attaches itself to living things and living things always die.

What you mean is that you are too wake for great destruction, so you just content yourself with small mischief, Faust retorts.

That may be true, Mephistopheles says. I admit I don't seem to be getting very far. So many men have died, taking the light with them, yet thousands of others always spring up to take their place.

Your trouble is that you don't take account of the ever-living power of creation, Faust says.

Perhaps, Mephistopheles replies. Let's argue about it some other time. Right now I would like your permission to go.

Why do you need my permission? Faust asks. You have the power to leave whenever you wish.

Mephistopheles explains that he was able to enter Faust's den only because a magic symbol drawn on the doorstep was not quite completed. But now that symbol keeps him from leaving, he says. And he cannot fly through the windows or up the chimney because devils have a rule that they must always level the way they came.

Well, now that I have you trapped, I think I'll keep you, Faust says. Mephistopheles pretends to agree to stay and then offers to show Faust some samples of his magic. Go right ahead, Faust says.

Mephistopheles calls forth a choir of spirits who sing a long, tender song about the beauties of nature and the bliss that man can attain. The song soothes Faust and he falls asleep.

Mephistopheles calls a rat forth from a hole in the wall and commands the rat to gnaw away the magic symbol. The rat does so and Mephistopheles is able to leave. As he steps through the door, he remarks that Faust is not yet a man able to hold a devil prisoner.

Faust's Study (lines 1530-2072)

The scene is the same as the previous one. It is the next day. Faust is alone in his study. Then Mephistopheles knocks on the door and steps into the room.

The Devil is dressed in fine red and gold clothes; he looks like a nobleman. He has a rooster feather in his hat and a sword at his side. I have come to cheer you up, Mephistopheles says. If you were dressed in clothes like these you would find what life can really be like.

No matter how I was dressed I would feel the pain of living, Faust replies. Then, in a magnificent speech, he says: "I am too old to be satisfied with just playing, and too young to be without ideas. What could the world reveal to me? All it says is 'You must renounce! You must renounce!' That's the eternal song everyone hears in his ears his whole life long. Every morning I wake up in terror: I could weep bitter tears to see the sun that runs its course easily but can do nothing to fulfill just one of my wishes-not one. If I even suspect that pleasure is near, the day is sure to scorn it. If I create a treasure with my mind, a thousand worldly caricatures pretend to see through it. And when night falls at last, I lie stretched fearful on my bed, and can get no rest, for wild dreams shake me. The god that lives in my heart will give me no peace and yet it can do nothing to control the world outside. Existence is a weight for me; I wish for death and hate life."

> Comment

This is a perfect summary of Faust's feelings. And it leads to the bargain that changes his unhappy life.

    Mephistopheles speaks. You say you want to die, and yet when death comes near, you do not welcome it. I remember you did not drink the poison from a certain bowl.

    You are quite an eavesdropper. Faust says.

    I don't know everything, but I see quite a lot, Mephistopheles replies. When I didn't drink that poison I was deceived, Faust says. Now I curse anything-possessions, a wife, wine, hope, or patience-that forces a man to live on in this world of illusion.

    An invisible choir of spirits breaks into song. You have shattered the beautiful world, it sings to Faust. Try to build a new one within yourself.

    Mephistopheles continues the song. You have shattered the song of the choir, he says. They are some of my lesser spirits, but they are right. You should try to start a new life, but not as a member of the common herd. If you agree, I will become your companion and bring you delight in your earthly existence. If you like, I will become your slave.

    And what do you want in return? Faust asks.

    Mephistopheles states the terms of the bargain: Here on earth I shall be your slave and work for you constantly. But after you die, you shall do the same for me.

I don't care what happens in the hereafter, Faust retorts. The only place I try to find joy is on the earth, and here I have found only disappointment.

Take my offer, Mephistopheles urges. I'll show you more than any man has seen before.

All I've found on earth is games that no one wins, Faust says. Gold runs away as soon as you get it, and even when you are lying with a girl you've seduced, she is ogling your best friend. Can you show me any fruit that doesn't rot before I pick it?

I will show you treasures that you can enjoy in peace, Mephistopheles promises.

Very well, says Faust. If ever I find relaxation on the earth, if ever I find delight in myself, then let death come. Then you may claim my soul. If at any moment I am so happy that I wish time to stand still, then I am your slave and you may take me. For I would have it no other way.

Done, says Mephistopheles. But remember the terms of our bargain as you have stated them, for I shall not forget.

Comment

Thus is the famous bargain made between Faust and the Devil. The terms are simple in their statement, although they will prove difficult to interpret in practice. Mephistopheles agrees to serve as Faust's servant in the world and to show him all earthly pleasures. In return, Faust agrees to serve as the Devil's servant after his death. Thus, in effect, Faust has sold his soul to the

Devil. However, we must keep in mind the important condition of the bargain-the condition on which the rest of the play turns: The Devil can only take Faust away to Hell when the doctor is completely satisfied for a moment with his life on earth. When Faust, in the midst of some pleasure, says to the moment "Wait, you are so fair," then he is dead and his soul belongs to the Devil. We must also remember the bet made earlier between Mephistopheles and God: The Devil contended he could capture Faust's soul but the Lord said that Faust was destined for Heaven. Thus, there are actually three principals in the bargain: 1) the Devil, waiting for Faust in Hell; 2) the Lord, waiting for him in Heaven; and 3) Faust himself, trying desperately to find joy in life on earth.

The agreement having been made verbally, Mephistopheles asks Faust for a written contract to make it legal.

Don't you trust me? Faust asks.

Don't get excited, the Devil says. Just sign the agreement with a drop of your blood. Faust does so.

Don't be afraid I'll go back on our bargain, Faust asserts. At one time I may have been committed to seeking knowledge on my own. But now I loathe knowledge; all I want is sensuality and passion. Since nature turned her back on me and the spirit would not stay at my command, the only thing that interests me is drinking my fill of pleasure.

You can have what you want, the Devil says. Help yourself.

I don't want simple, pure joy, says Faust. I want excesses; I want leaping bliss and deepest agony.

I want my existence to be uncontrolled. For this is the kind of activity that shows what a man is.

I shall do what I can, Mephistopheles replies. But you must always remember that you are a man and not a god. Come, let us leave this place of grief and fly out into the world. Let's leave this school, for what I shall show you would not be suitable to be taught to students. In fact, I think I hear one of them in the hall now.

I can't face the boy, Faust says.

Give me your cap and gown, says Mephistopheles. I'll dress up like you. In the meantime, you get ready for our trip.

Mephistopheles dresses in Faust's clothes and Faust leaves the room. A student enters; he is young and unsure of himself.

I have just arrived here, the student says bashfully, and I have come to see the famous intellectual, Dr. Faust.

Well here I am, Mephistopheles says. And you see I am a man just like anyone else.

I am a sincere student, the young man says. I beg you to take me under your wing and teach me. I have some spare cash and I am cheerful, and there is much I hope to learn.

Then this is the place for you, Mephistopheles says.

To tell you the truth, I'm a little afraid of it, the student replies. The room seems so gloomy, and there is not one touch of green to show that there is some living thing around. When I go to hear a lecture, my brain gets numb.

Comment

This scene between the young student and Mephistopheles pretending to be the learned Dr. Faust is an interlude in the action of the play. The scene is a clever comment on pedantry in education, particularly on education as it was practiced in the sixteenth century. At that time, learning was a stuffy affair. Independent thinking was out of the question; the student was expected to learn the authorized doctrine and repeat it by rote. When examples were needed to prove a point in the doctrine, they were taken from books or old legends. The real world was not considered in teaching. The scholar was expected to live in isolation from nature and from the cares and joys of existence in the world. This isolation is what the student refers to when he says that there isn't a spot of green in the classroom. Mephistopheles will have several biting remarks to make about this method of education, remarks applicable to education in any century, not only the sixteenth.

You will get used to the gloomy surroundings and the lack of nature, Mephistopheles says, as would any teacher in the system. What do you want to major in? Mephistopheles asks the confused student.

I want to know everything, the student replies.

Then let me tell you how to go about it, Mephistopheles says. (We should remember that Mephistopheles is speaking here not as the Devil but as the pedantic Dr. Faust. He is really making fun of the methods he pretends to describe.) First of all, you must study hard, for time is short, the Devil says. You begin with logic. That is the science that makes simple things hard. Eating and drinking, which you once knew intuitively and accepted without question, will become complex operations when logical principles are applied to them. You must take things step by step and then analyze each step. Then, when all the actions of life are broken down into separate steps, you can begin to put them together again and become an honored philosopher. You will hold all the pieces of life in the palm of your hand. You will lack nothing except the human spirit that holds them together and makes them live. Thus you will be making a fool of yourself and not even realize it.

I am thoroughly confused, the poor student says.

Don't worry, says Mephistopheles, it will all become clear to you with study. After you have mastered logic, you can turn your attention to metaphysics. That is the science of cramming into a man's brain more than he was meant to understand. But you won't have to worry about understanding it, for you can always talk your way out with some high-sounding phrase.

And don't forget the rules here, Mephistopheles goes on. Spend five hours a day studying, and read your books carefully. Then you will see that all the wisdom your teacher pretends to give you actually comes from the same books you read. But write down everything he says anyway.

You are right, the student says. It's a good idea to write everything down. Then you have something to take home with you.

But you must choose a field of concentration, Mephistopheles says.

Well, law doesn't appeal to me, replies the student.

I don't blame you, the Devil says. The laws of a country seem to me to be some disease carried over from generation to generation. They do not take account of the changing times. What once was wisdom becomes nonsense.

How about theology? the student asks.

There are many roads in theology that lead to error, Mephistopheles answers. The best way to approach it is to have only one teacher, and follow everything he says no matter what anyone else tells you. But here again it is a matter of words and not deeds.

Isn't there anything? the student says. How about medicine?

Here Mephistopheles undergoes a change. I am tired of pretending to be a pedant, he says to himself. I will now speak again as the Devil. You can study science all you like, the Devil says to the undergraduate, but it won't do you much good. The thing to do is to place your trust in momentary pleasure. And medicine is a good way to gain pleasure if you take advantage of it. For if you act sincere, your patients, especially the women, will have confidence in you. Women will come to you with a thousand complaints, but they can all be cured with one simple act. When they come to see you for treatment, the first thing to do is take off all their clothes and examine their bodies carefully with your hands. Some people have to wait years to get as far with them as you can in one visit.

Medicine seems like the profession for me, the student says.

Suddenly Mephistopheles' playful mood changes. My friend, he says to the student, all theories are gray. The only thing that's green is life itself.

Before I go, would you sign my album? the student says.

Mephistopheles takes the book and writes in it in Latin: "Eritis sicut Deus, scientes bonum et malum" (You will be like a god, and come to know good and evil). Follow that ancient text and you will soon find yourself in terror, the Devil says.

Comment

Mephistopheles here presents the argument we have already seen embodied in the words of Dr. Faust. When a man seeks to know everything, he is trying to be like God. Among the things he will try to learn is the difference between good and evil, which was the original cause for the fall of man in the Garden of Eden and the reason for his unhappy life on earth. Man is thus doomed to unhappiness because of his attempt to be like God. This is how Mephistopheles sees man's unhappy lot, and he sees no alternative for it. At the end of the play, an alternative is found, one that the Devil doesn't know about.

The student leaves and Faust re-enters the room.

Where are we going? he asks Mephistopheles.

Wherever you like, the Devil says. We shall see the world and have fun.

I shall be shy in the world, Faust says. I always have been. I always feel so small in the presence of others.

You'll feel differently when you gain self-confidence, the Devil says.

How shall we go where we're going? Faust asks. Do you have a carriage waiting?

No, we can fly, Mephistopheles answers. It's faster. And, by the way congratulations on your new life.

Faust and Mephistopheles leave, and the scene closes.

Comment

Already Mephistopheles has taken away from Faust one of the prides of his life-his fame as a teacher. Faust has allowed the Devil to play his part. The doctor will give much more to Mephistopheles before the play is over.

Auerbach's Keller (lines 2073-2336)

Auerbach's Keller (Keller is German for cellar) is a tavern in the city of Leipzig in eastern Germany. As the scene opens we find four men (Frosch, Brander, Siebel, and Altmayer) indulging in a drinking bout.

Frosch is the first to speak. Why are there no laughing and drinking? he asks. You all look like wet dishrags.

Brander answers. It's all your fault. You are not making any jokes or playing tricks on us the way you usually do.

Frosch picks up a glass of wine and pours it over Brander's head. In this the kind of joke you like? he asks.

Brander is angry. You filthy pig, he says.

Now Siebel joins in. No fighting, he says. Let's all drink up and sing some loud songs.

This is where I leave, Altmayer says jokingly. Give me some cotton to stuff in my ears.

The four drinking companions sing snatches of songs and then comment on them, talking of politics, religion, and love. Finally Brander pounds his glass on the table for attention. Listen to this song, he says, and sings about a rat who lived happily in a cellar, eating his fill, until one day the cook poisoned him. While the rat was dying of the poison it looked as if he were enjoying the convulsions of love, the song went. All join in on the chorus: "As if his body were full of love." The men talk some more and exchange further insults.

At this point, Faust and Mephistopheles enter the tavern. This is what you need more than anything else, the Devil says to the doctor. A little jolly company to see that life can be fun. These fellows here make every day a holiday. As long as they have credit and are not suffering from a hangover, they have fun.

Brander spots the pair who has entered. Those are visitors to our city, he says. I can tell by the way they stare at us.

It's no wonder, Frosch replies. For Leipzig is widely known as a tourist spot. Many people call it the "Little Paris."

The men speculate about the identity of the two strangers. Frosch thinks they are noblemen and Brander thinks they are poor quack doctors. They decide to buy the strangers a drink and pump them. Mephistopheles hears the conversation. You see how people are, he says to Faust. The Devil might be right next to them but they never know it.

The strangers join the four drinking companions. Siebel looks sideways at Mephistopheles and whispers to his companions: What's the matter with this fellow? He seems to be limping on one foot.

Comment

Siebel's remark is a reference to a legend about the Devil. The Devil is able to appear in human form except for one cloven hoof instead of a foot. This misshapen foot, in the form of a goat's hoof, points to the animal origins of the Devil.

The group talks, and Mephistopheles proves to be better than they are at exchanging insults. Faust says nothing, aside from one sentence, for the rest of the scene.

Mephistopheles offers to sing a song. The men ask for something they have not heard before. Mephistopheles agrees and sings an amusing song about a flea. It seems that once a long time ago a king adopted a flea and made him a minister of the court. He dressed the flea in the finest clothes and gave him tiny medals and decorations. Soon, all the flea's relatives also became members of the king's court. All of the lords and ladies of the court, including the queen herself, were eaten alive by the fleas and grew very thin. But no one was allowed to kill the bugs because they were protected by the king. We are much more fortunate because we can kill all the fleas we catch.

Everyone except Faust joins in the chorus: "But we can crack them and crush them anytime they bite."

The drinkers are very pleased with the song. Altmayer offers a toast: Long live freedom and long live wine, he says. I would like to join the toast, Mephistopheles says, but I can't. I'm all for freedom but your wine is very bad. If I weren't afraid the owner would protest, I would offer you something to drink from my own cellar.

Go ahead, Siebel says. The owner is an ass.

Very well, Mephistopheles says. Bring me a drill. When he gets the drill the devil asks Frosch what kind of wine he would like.

Frosch is surprised. Surely you don't carry a wine cellar around with you! he says. Mephistopheles answers: Just tell me what kind you want.

I'll have some Rhine wine, Frosch says, for I am always loyal to the Fatherland.

Mephistopheles drills a hole in the top of the table before Frosch and then puts a cork in it. Is this some kind of parlor trick? Altmayer asks. Mephistopheles addresses Brander. Brander wants champagne. Mephistopheles repeats the procedure with the drill. Siebel asks for Tokay and Altmayer says it doesn't make any difference to him, everything tastes good.

When all the holes are bored and filled with stoppers, Mephistopheles makes some gestures and repeats a magic formula. The four men pull out the stoppers and their glasses are filled with the kinds of wine they requested. They all drink several times and sing about how happy they feel.

Now you see how happy men are when they are free, Mephistopheles says to Faust. The doctor can only say: I would like to get out of here. We'll go soon, the Devil replies, but first watch how like animals men can get.

The men are quite drunk by this time. Siebel spills some of his wine on the floor and it turns into a flame. He is terrified. Mephistopheles makes some magic gestures and the flame subsides. That was only a drop of purgatory, he says to Siebel.

Siebel is angry at the trick. Don't try that again, he says. The others join in and warn Mephistopheles.

Altmayer pulls a stopper out of the table and flames shoot up. It's some unholy magic, Siebel says. He must be an outlaw; we must kill him. The four drinkers draw their knives and advance on the Devil.

Mephistopheles repeats a spell and the attackers suddenly feel that they are in some strange beautiful land that abounds with grapes. Brander grabs Siebel by the nose; Altmayer does the same with Frosch.

Mephistopheles commands the illusion to disappear. Remember how the Devil plays tricks, he says to the four men. Then he and Faust vanish. The revelers let go of each other's noses. They are terrified and do not quite know what has happened to them.

Who was that trickster? Siebel asks. I saw him zoom right out of the door on a barrel, Altmayer says. My feet feel like lead from fear. Let no one say there are no miracles in the world today, Altmayer concludes. The scene closes.

Comment

Thus Mephistopheles has given Faust a taste of low life. Faust obviously did not like it, for he barely spoke during the whole scene. But the doctor has been acquainted with dissipation as it is practiced on earth. In the next scene, he will enter the supernatural realm. But notice how similar the scenes are in their setting and form.

PART 3

Witch's Kitchen (lines 2337-2604)

A large kettle boils over a low fire in the middle of the room. Steam rises from it. A female monkey sits near the kettle, tending it. A male monkey sits next to the female with their young. He is warming himself. The walls and ceiling of the room are decorated with the strange instruments of witchcraft. Faust and Mephistopheles enter the room.

Faust speaks. How I hate this sorcery, he says. How can I be made whole in this mess? How can these animals reduce my age by thirty years? Isn't there somewhere in the world where I can find a cure that is not as filthy as this?

My friend, Mephistopheles says, there is only one other way that you could become young. But that is another story.

Tell me, Faust says.

All right, Mephistopheles says, but I warn you that it does not involve magic. You don't need a doctor or money either. Just go out into the fields and dig. Lead a simple life and eat simple food. Live close to the land. Then you will find that at eighty you are still young.

I am not used to that life, Faust says. That kind of farming life is too narrow for me.

Then you see that we need witchcraft, Mephistopheles retorts.

All right, Faust says. But with all your power can't you find someone cleaner than these monkeys?

I can't waste my time on that kind of thing, the Devil says. I am the inspiration for all their doings, but I myself cannot be bothered with all that mess. And besides, look how delicate they look. That is the maid and that is the butler.

Then Mephistopheles speaks to the monkeys. It seems that your mistress is not at home.

The monkeys answer, She has gone away to fly through the sky.

And how long will she fly? the Devil asks.

As long as we warm our feet, the monkeys reply.

The male monkey crawls up to Mephistopheles' feet. Please let us get rich, the monkey says. Then we might find rest.

You see, Mephistopheles says to Faust, even the monkeys think they will be happy if they could only get rich.

While this conversation has been going on, Faust has been looking in a mirror on the wall. In the mirror is the image of a beautiful young girl. Can I ever see such a lovely creature on the earth? Faust asks. I have never seen anything so beautiful.

If I work hard I could get you such a woman, Mephistopheles says. Wouldn't it be nice to have such a girl and make her your own for life? he says to Faust. If you could marry her, your life would be complete.

All this time the monkeys have been capering around Faust and the Devil.

Faust, looking into the mirror at the fair image, says: I think I will go mad.

Mephistopheles, watching the prancing monkeys, says the same thing.

Comment

This is the first step in the Devil's campaign to make Faust completely happy. We must remember the terms of the bargain between them: If at any moment Faust is so happy that he says to the moment "Wait, you are so fair," then he must accept death and give over his soul to the Devil. Here in this scene we see a definite attempt by Mephistopheles to achieve this moment. Faust is enticed by the image he sees in the mirror. The Devil is busy preparing the way for the doctor to meet the image in real life.

While the monkeys have been running around and talking to the Devil, the kettle the female is supposed to be watching runs over. A flame leaps up through the chimney when it spills, and the witch appears through the flame making a terrific din.

The witch curses the monkey for letting the pot run over. Then she sees Faust and Mephistopheles. The witch is annoyed at their presence and tries to drive them away with flames from the boiling kettle.

Mephistopheles makes some gestures and repeats a spell, and the witch's implements are broken in two. The witch retreats in terror.

Now do you recognize me? Mephistopheles asks. Don't you know your master when you see him?

Forgive my uncouth greeting, the witch says, but you do not look like the Devil I knew formerly.

Culture is everywhere now and it even extends to the Devil, Mephistopheles replies. I have done away with the horns and tail and claws that people used to see in the Devil. I still have this one cloven foot, but that I can conceal by padding.

The witch dances around in a frenzy. Satan is back! Satan is back! she sings.

Don't call me Satan, Mephistopheles says. That name is dated too. Men associate it with fables. I am a gentleman of noble background. If you doubt it, have a look at my coat of arms (the Devil makes an indecent gesture).

The witch laughs uproariously. That was always your way, sir, she says. You were always a jester.

This is the way witches like to be treated, Mephistopheles says to Faust. Then the Devil turns to the witch again when she asks him why he is visiting her. We have come for a glass of your magic brew, the strongest kind, Mephistopheles says.

I have a bottle of the best right here on the shelf, the witch says. But make sure your companion is prepared for it, or else he will die instantly.

This man is a friend of mine and he will take the potion well, the Devil answers. Now get your tools of magic together and let's get on with it.

The witch draws a circle on the floor and puts various strange implements in it. Then she gets a large book. One of the monkeys holds it for her; the other holds a torch.

Do we have to go through all this hocus-pocus? Faust asks. I have long practiced this kind of thing and I know what a fraud it is.

Don't be so serious, the Devil replies. Join in the fun. The witch then begins to recite a spell from the book involving a lot of numbers. She calls it "witch's arithmetic."

This is nonsense, Faust says. Of course it is, Mephistopheles retorts. But it has an honored history. Men have always been intrigued by strange spells and illusions, and even sages have taken it up at one time or another. Men seem to believe that if they hear words there must be some sort of meaning behind them.

Comment

This sharp comment of Mephistopheles' is directed at all the scholars, philosophers, and theologians who think that words themselves will relate a vague idea to real life. It is one of the many biting remarks the Devil makes about fraudulent scholarship in the play. While Mephistopheles is in a certain sense an anti-intellectual (he believes that God-given reason is the cause of man's unhappiness), in another sense he is the supreme user of reason, for he uses it to see through many of the illusions of life.

But enough of this, Mephistopheles says to the witch. Give my friend the potion to drink. It will not hurt him.

Faust puts the cup to his lips as flames leap from it. He drinks. We have to get going, the Devil says. We cannot rest until that potion is absorbed in your body. Later on we will have lots of leisure, but now we must make you sweat and let the drink's power work out through your skin. Soon you will have plenty of pleasure, when Cupid shoots his arrows into you.

Just let me look into the mirror once more, Faust pleads. I want to see that beautiful form again.

Not now, Mephistopheles commands. Before you know it you will see a woman in the flesh who is as beautiful as that illusion. And then softly the Devil says: With the help of that potion, every woman will look like Helen of Troy to you.

Comment

Thus the Devil has restored Faust's youthful spirits and prepared him for the love affair that will occupy most of the remaining first part of the tragedy. The once old and dispirited Dr. Faust is ready to fall in love as few men have done before.

Since we shall meet Helen of Troy later, in the second part of the play, it would be well to refresh our memories now as to her identity. Helen was the wife of Menelaus, the king of Sparta in Greece. Menelaus's brother, Agamemnon, was the king of Achaea and the leader of the Greek warlords. Paris, one of the many sons of the king of Troy in Asia Minor, visited the court of Menelaus and fell in love with Helen. Paris took Helen back with him to Troy. Agamemnon called the Greeks together and led them on an expedition to Troy to regain his brother's wife. This was the beginning of the famous Trojan War, of which Helen was the cause. According to legend, Helen was one of the most beautiful women who ever lived. In classical times and after, her name was always a synonym for beauty.

Street (lines 2605-2677)

Faust and Mephistopheles return to the real world. The scene is the street of an ordinary German town. Faust is walking alone as Margaret, a simple and pure girl, passes by.

Fair lady, may I offer to walk you home? Faust says to the girl.

I am neither fair nor am I a lady, Margaret replies, and can get home quite well without your help. The girl takes her arm out of Faust's grasp and walks away.

I have never seen a girl as fair as that, Faust says. She is obviously virtuous, but she is not shy either. What ecstasy!

Mephistopheles enters. Get me that girl, Faust commands. I'm not sure that I can, the Devil replies slyly. She has just been to see her confessor and has a spotless conscience. You seem to think that girls are just waiting around for you to pick them.

If you don't comply with my wish and if that girl does not lie in my arms this very night, then we shall part company and our bargain is off, Faust threatens.

At least give me some time, Mephistopheles says. Fourteen days at least.

If I had seven hours alone with her I would not even need the Devil's help to seduce her, Faust retorts.

You talk just like a Frenchman, Mephistopheles says. Wouldn't it be better to put off your pleasure for a while, so you can enjoy it bit by bit?

I have enough appetite for her without dragging it out, Faust says.

Well, we'll never get her by direct assault, Mephistopheles says. We shall have to use trickery.

At least take me to her room, Faust begs. Get me some memento of her-a handkerchief or a garter.

I will take you to her room today, Mephistopheles says.

And shall I see her? Faust asks. Shall I have her?

No, not yet, the Devil answers. She has to visit a neighbor. However, you can sit in her chamber and dream of future pleasures.

Then get me a present I can leave for her, Faust says.

I know a nice place where there is lots of buried treasure, Mephistopheles says. I will get you a present for her.

Evening (lines 2678-2804)

The scene is Margaret's small, neat room. Margaret is alone, braiding her hair.

I would like to know who that gentleman was today who accosted me on the street, Margaret says to herself. He looked very gallant and he appeared to be of noble family. For it is known that noblemen are very bold with ladies. Then Margaret leaves on her visit to a neighbor.

Mephistopheles and Faust enter the room. After a short silence Faust asks the Devil to leave him alone. Mephistopheles complies.

Faust launches into a long soliloquy. What a sense of calm I feel here, he says. Even though the surroundings are not rich and opulent, there seems to be an air of order and complete content. My love's hand is godlike, for it can make a cottage seem like Heaven. And yet I am so deeply moved. I feel so strange. My heart is heavy with love. I don't even know myself anymore.

Mephistopheles rushes back into the room. Let's go, he says, she's coming back.

Come on, Faust says. I shall never come back again.

Comment

This is the first premonition of the tragedy to come. Faust realizes that if he pursues his designs on Margaret with the Devil's help, he can only bring harm to her. He cares so much for her that he wants to go away and leave her as pure and untroubled as when he found her. However, he will change his mind, although reluctantly.

Before they leave, Mephistopheles places a case of jewels he has collected in Margaret's closet.

Margaret re-enters the room with a lamp. The room seems suddenly sultry to her and she opens the window. I feel so strange, she says. I wish my mother would get home.

As she undresses, she sings a simple song about king in Thule. It is one of Goethe's most famous poems. The king, she sings, had a golden goblet that his mistress gave him when he died. He took great joy in drinking from it, for it always brought back her memory. When he was near death, he gave everything in his kingdom to his heir except the goblet. On the last day of his life the old king took one final drink from the goblet and threw it into the sea. Then he died. That is the end of the song.

Then Margaret discovers the jewels. She is puzzled at their being there but tries some of them on. She is pleased at the way she looks with them. Beauty and goodness do not get anyone very far, she says. Everything really depends on how much gold and jewels you have. Pity on the poor, she concludes.

Promenade (lines 2805-2864)

Faust is walking up and down, lost in his thoughts of Margaret. Mephistopheles enters cursing.

What is the matter? Faust asks.

A dirty priest has got the whole set of jewels we gave to Margaret, Mephistopheles says. The girl showed them to her mother, and her mother, being a religious woman, immediately sensed that something was wrong. So they brought the jewels to the Church as an offering. The Church has a big appetite: She has gobbled up whole countries, but still has a little room left over in her stomach for smaller things.

Comment

This passage illustrates Goethe's dislike of the organized Church. Although the conclusion of the play is essentially a religious one, it has nothing to do with the redeeming power of any church. Goethe believed that man's salvation depends on man's own efforts and his personal relationship with God. The poet despised the Church and put many satirical remarks about it in the mouths of his characters.

And what about Gretchen? asks Faust. How did she take the loss of the jewels? (Gretchen is the nickname form of Margaret in German. The two names, Gretchen and Margaret, are used interchangeably in the play.)

She is uneasy about it, the devil replies, She mopes about and doesn't know what to do. And, most of all, she wonders who gave the gems to her.

My darling's grief distresses me, Faust says. Get some more jewels to replace the ones she has lost. And while you're at it you might try to find out who the neighbor is that Margaret visits.

Mephistopheles agrees. After Faust leaves he says: A fool in love doesn't care about practical things. If he had to destroy the sun and moon and all the stars, he would do it to further his love.

The Neighbor's House (lines 2865-3024)

The scene is the house of Martha Schwerdtlein. Martha is the friend and confidante of Margaret. We find Martha alone, lamenting the disappearance of her husband. It seems that he went off in the world to seek his fortune and has not been heard of since. If he is dead, I wish I had at least a certificate to that effect, Martha says.

Margaret enters the room. She is very excited, for she has found another collection of jewels in her closet. Don't tell your mother or she will give them to the priest, too, Martha advises. Margaret agrees.

Comment

Mephistopheles is beginning to have his way with the girl. She is beginning to lose her good and simple ways. Unfortunately, she will lose much more before the Devil is through with her.

There is a knock at the door and Mephistopheles enters. Forgive the intrusion, he says, but I am looking for Martha Schwerdtlein. What do you want? Martha asks. I want to talk to you but I do not want to disturb this elegant gathering, he answers. Perhaps I can come back when the noble lady has left.

Mephistopheles' false flattery has some effect on Margaret. I am nothing but a poor young maid, she says. These jewels are not mine. It's not only the jewels, Mephistopheles says slyly. Everything about you indicates you are a lady of noble birth.

Then the Devil turns his attention to Martha. He concocts a story about knowing her husband. Her husband is dead, he says; he is buried in Padua, Italy, in St. Anthony's churchyard.

Martha is upset at the news. She asks Mephistopheles if he has brought any memento of her husband or any part of the treasure he is supposed to have accumulated during his adventures.

Mephistopheles continues to weave his lying tale. He tells Martha that her husband did accumulate some riches but that he squandered them all on a girl in Naples. But on his deathbed the husband thought of Martha and asked her forgiveness, the Devil says.

The rogue, exclaims Martha. I deserved better than that, for I was always faithful to him.

Then the Devil flatters Martha. If I were you, I would wait a year and then remarry, he says. But in the meantime a handsome woman like you should have no trouble finding a lover. I myself, for example, find you extremely attractive. Then the Devil prepares to leave.

Not so fast, Martha says. I need a certificate of my husband's death. That is the only way I will be free to remarry.

Very well, Mephistopheles says. As you know, anything that is sworn to by two witnesses is considered true. I have a splendid friend who will appear with me before the magistrate. With our testimony, you can easily get a certificate.

Martha agrees to the arrangement, and invites the Devil and his friend to meet her in her garden in the evening.

Will that charming lady be there too? he asks, pointing to Margaret. For my friend is a gallant and likes the ladies.

I would have to blush before him, Margaret says.

You do not have to blush before anybody, not even a king, Mephistopheles replies.

We shall expect you and your friend tonight then, Martha says, in the garden behind my house.

PART 4

Street (lines 3025-3072)

Faust and Mephistopheles meet. How is it going? asks Faust. Very well, the Devil replies. I see you are on fire with expectation. You will see Gretchen later this afternoon at Martha's. That woman (Martha) seems especially made to help out a pimp.

But we must do something in return for the meeting, the Devil says. You must go before a judge with me and swear that Martha's husband is buried in Padua.

That was not very clever of you, Faust says. For now we will have to go to Padua and make sure he is buried there.

What a holy man you are! Mephistopheles says. Do you mean you have never testified to something that was not true? How about all the times you lectured to your students and knew nothing more about the subject than they did? Wouldn't you call that perjury?

You are a false philosopher and a liar, Faust retorts.

And won't you swear undying love to Gretchen? Mephistopheles continues. And won't that be perjury too? Because tomorrow you will deceive her.

I will swear love to her, but it will be with all my heart, Faust replies. My senses are reeling from my love for her.

That may very well be true, Mephistopheles says, but you will not even see her unless you agree to my plan.

All right, let's go to the judge, Faust says. You are right, but the only reason you are right is that I have no choice.

Comment

Thus, Faust takes another step on the road to Hell. First we saw him give up his sacred teaching duties to the Devil. Then we saw him participate in rioting and revelry. Now Mephistopheles has convinced him to commit perjury. But, like Gretchen, Faust has many more troubles and evil acts still in store for him. These will make the previous ones seem like child's play to him.

Garden (lines 3073–3204)

The scene is the garden behind Martha's house. Two couples, Margaret and Faust and Martha and Mephistopheles, stroll back and forth across the stage. We hear snatches of conversation first from one couple and then from the other.

Faust and Margaret walk by. Margaret has her hand on Faust's arm. I think you are just being kind to me, Margaret says. I don't have much to say that would interest a traveling gentleman like you.

One look from you gives me more pleasure than all the world's wisdom, Faust replies. He kisses Gretchen's hand.

How could you kiss my hand? Margaret asks. It is so rough and ugly from the hard work I have to do. I am constantly busy tending to the needs of my mother.

The couple passes, and Mephistopheles and Martha take their place. Mephistopheles tells the supposed widow that he must keep traveling in search of adventure. Martha advises him to settle down, presumably with her.

Faust and Margaret reappear. Are you often lonely? Faust asks the girl.

Often, Gretchen replies. I have to do all the work for my mother, as we have no cook or maid. And my mother is very particular that I do the housework properly. It's not that we are poor; my father left us some money and the house. But my days are plain. My brother is a soldier and the little sister I once loved is dead.

Martha is flirting with the Devil. It is hard for me to convince you of the need for a home and a family, she says. If you are alert you might, Mephistopheles answers.

Faust and Gretchen return.

You recognized me as I came into the garden, Faust says. I hope you will forgive my free behavior with you the other day when you left the church.

At first I was upset, Margaret replies. But then another feeling grew within me and I wasn't angry anymore.

Margaret picks a daisy and plays he-loves-me-he-loves-me-not. When she pulls out the last petal, she says. "He loves me." Faust takes her two hands in his and tells her of his love and rapture. Margaret clasps his hands for a moment, then breaks away and runs. Faust follows.

Martha and Mephistopheles enter the scene again. Martha is trying to convince him of the benefits of living in her town. Then they discuss the other couple. It looks as if he is talking to her, Martha says. That's the way the world goes, Mephistopheles replies.

A Bower In The Garden (lines 3205-3216)

The scene is a sheltered place in Martha's garden. The time is immediately after the preceding scene.

Margaret leaps into the bower and hides behind the door. Then she peeks out. He is coming, she says.

Faust enters. You are teasing me, he says. Then the kisses the girl.

Gretchen embraces him and returns his kiss. Dearest man, I love you with all my heart, she says.

Mephistopheles knocks at the door. Who is that? Faust asks angrily. It's time to go, the Devil says. Martha enters. Yes, it is late, she adds.

Can't I take you home? Faust asks Gretchen.

No, my mother would object, replies the girl. But come again soon. Faust and Mephistopheles leave.

He is a wonderful man, Margaret says. I cannot find any answer for him except "Yes." I am a simple girl, and I cannot guess what he sees in me.

Wood And Cave (lines 3217–3373)

Faust has run away from Gretchen's town so that he will not ruin the girl's life. We find him alone in a wild place.

Faust is giving thanks to the gods for his happy state. He thanks them for giving him the experience of natural love. He is pleased that he was allowed not only to see Margaret but also to converse with her and look into her heart. He also thanks the gods for the self-enlightening that the experience has given him. But he realizes that his experience is not perfect, for he has to travel with the Devil. Mephistopheles is a necessity now to him, Faust says, even though he makes all his joys seem small and belittles the works of the gods.

> Comment

It is ironic that Faust is thanking God for the gifts that Mephistopheles has brought him. But we must remember what God said at the beginning of the play: Faust is his servant. Although Faust will take many wrong roads and do many evil deeds, he will eventually find his way home to God. This statement of the Lord's is borne out by Faust's speech.

Mephistopheles enters the scene. Haven't you had enough of the solitary life? the Devil asks. Don't you long for something new?

I wish you had something else to do besides pester me, Faust replies.

I shall leave if you like, the Devil says. An unpleasant fellow like you would hardly be a loss to Hell. He continues: if I had left you alone, do you think you would be in the exalted state you're in? I saved you from suicide. And now you sit like an old owl in the wilderness, still not cured of your scholastic nonsense.

I am enjoying my reverie, Faust says.

You may think you are enjoying yourself, the Devil replies. But it is just a substitute for sexual intercourse. No matter how chaste you may think you are, there is no one who can do without that in one form or another.

Gretchen is unhappy because you have gone, the Devil continues. She sits at her window and loves you to the breaking point. It seems to me that instead of sitting here brooding, you should give the poor thing her reward and go to bed with her.

Damnable fiend, Faust cries. You are leading me back to lust for her.

That is good, Mephistopheles replies. God was not so dumb when he made lust a part of the human equipment.

What a wretched man I am, Faust says in despair. And yet I cannot control myself, I must have her and smash her life. So let us go onward. What is to be must be. Let her fate be on my head. Let her perish with me.

Go back to her, Mephistopheles says. If you had held out against your desire you would be a god. But since you cannot resist, you are a devil. And there is nothing in the world more absurd than a devil who is in despair. If you cannot be a godlike man, then be a devil with all your might.

Comment

Mephistopheles has won over Dr. Faust once more. And yet somehow we are not surprised. The play is we know, a tragedy and all the events seem to lead inevitably to a final doom. We must realize, at least subconsciously, that if Faust had given up his lust for Gretchen there would be no play and no tragedy.

Gretchen's Room (lines 3374-3413)

Margaret is sitting at the spinning wheel in her room. She is alone and in despair, for she thinks Faust is gone. She sings a simple and beautiful song. The song has become one of Goethe's best-loved poems:

Peace has left, My heart is sore; I shall find it never, Ah, nevermore.

Gretchen sings on. Unless he is near, the world seems like a grave to me. I sit at my window and look out for him. I long for the touch of his hand and his kiss. I wish I could embrace him once more. I would kiss him to my heart's content, until in his kisses I was spent.

Comment

This simple and lyrical scene shows Goethe's genius and economy as a playwright. The scene lasts no more than five minutes, and yet we could not know more about Gretchen's state of mind if it went on for an hour. In fact, in the whole description of Faust's love affair with Gretchen, not one word is wasted. We are shown the essential things; the rest is left to our imaginations.

Martha's Garden (lines 3414-3543)

We find Margaret and Faust in the garden where they have been before.

Margaret is trying to make Faust promise that he will be a more religious man. She asks him if he believes in God.

Who would dare say that there is no God? Faust replies. It is obvious that there is something that embraces and sustains the world.

Is there not some order in nature? Is there not some supernatural joy in love? It is just that I believe that when you try to apply words to this supreme power, you cloud the issue.

I fear you are not a Christian, though, Gretchen says. For your companion makes me afraid. He mocks everything. When I am with you, I feel warm and free, but when he comes these feelings are strangled.

That is just because you dislike the man, Faust replies. There must also be some eccentrics in the world, you know.

Margaret says she must go. Faust stops her. Isn't there any time when we can lie and rest together? he asks.

If I lived alone I would do it, Gretchen says. But my mother is not a sound sleeper and if she ever caught me at it I would die.

Here, Faust says. Take this bottle and pour three drops of the liquid in your mother's drink. Then she will not wake up easily.

I will do it, Gretchen says. I have done so much for you already I cannot deny you more.

Comment

Faust does not know it, but this is a fatal step for him. The bottle that Mephistopheles has given him does not contain a sleeping potion. It contains a poison that will kill Gretchen's mother.

Gretchen leaves the garden and Mephistopheles enters. Is she gone? the Devil asks. You were eavesdropping, Faust asserts.

Why not? the Devil says. And I hope you got religion through her lesson.

You are a monster, Faust says, but you shall never gain control of her pure soul.

You are a fool to let a maiden lead you by the nose, Mephistopheles retorts. But she has a certain cleverness, for she perceives that I am evil. Maybe she thinks I am the Devil. But tonight we shall see how you make out.

That's no business of yours, Faust says.

I get some pleasure from it too, Mephistopheles says as the scene ends.

At The Well (lines 3544-3586)

Gretchen and Lieschen, a young girl who is a friend of Gretchen's, meet at the city well. Both have jugs at their hips; they have come to draw water.

Lieschen tells Gretchen about Barbara, a girl in the town who has been made pregnant by her lover. It stinks, Lieschen says. When she eats and drinks now, she is feeding two. But that is what she deserves. She followed him around and took his presents and flirted with him. And now she is a maid no more.

The poor thing, Gretchen sighs.

She doesn't deserve pity, Lieschen retorts. When girls like us were home with our mothers and our spinning wheels every night, she was out in the town enjoying the attention of her lover. She should do penance now like any sinner.

Comment

Lieschen is a perfect example of the plain girl who begrudges to others what she cannot have herself. In just a few lines Goethe presents us with a complete portrait of that kind of woman.

> Perhaps her lover will marry her, says Gretchen.

FAUST

TEXTUAL ANALYSIS

PART TWO

ACT ONE

Pleasant Landscape (lines 4613–4727)

Faust is stretched out in a flowery meadow. He is weary and restless and longs for sleep. Twilight has just fallen. A ring of Spirits swirls around him in graceful movement. Ariel, one of the spirits, sings a soothing song to the accompaniment of harps.

Soothe the storm of Faust's mortal heart, Ariel sings to the Spirits. Wash away the memory of horrors past and give him comfort. Renew his strength through sleep and lead him back to the air of Heaven.

A choir continues Ariel's beautiful song. Breathe renewed faith, for your illness is past, the choir sings. Rise with the dawn, your will unclouded and your conscience unspotted.

Comment

We see immediately that the second part of the play will be different from the first. The pace is more relaxed and the presence of evil is less evident. Whereas in the first part we followed Faust at breakneck speed through a series of intensely dramatic scenes culminating with the Gretchen-tragedy, we will find him in this part wandering for most of his time into the classical past. The romantic emphasis on storm and stress, deep passion, the agony of existence will be replaced by the classical emphasis on calm, refinement, and intellect. Even the poetry has changed. The lines are looser and flow more easily, while in the first part they thundered or twisted with despair and passion. If the first part was written from the heart, the second part comes from the intellect.

The dawn breaks and Faust awakes after a restful sleep. I feel clothed afresh in the joy of living and the wonder of the earth, Faust says. The world in all its shining beauty seems like paradise to me. The sun is so dazzling I must turn and refresh my eyes at the waterfall. Here the cataract crashes on the boulders, sending up a rainbow in the vapor. The life of mortal man is like this; he has his being in the reflections and changing hues of nature.

Imperial Palace: (lines 4728–5064)

The scene is the throne room of a splendid court. The Council of State, dressed in fine costumes, is awaiting the arrival of the Emperor.

The Emperor arrives with his retinue and takes the throne. Where is my jester? he asks. He is told that the court fool has fallen down the steps, either because he was drunk or because of some terrible accident.

Mephistopheles steps forward and asks the Emperor a riddle, the answer to which is "the Devil." However, the Emperor says he has no time for riddles and instead asks Mephistopheles to be his new jester. Mephistopheles goes up to the throne and takes his place at the left hand of the monarch.

The Emperor says that with his splendid court he is reluctant to turn his attention to the practical problems of running a state. However, he bids his officials report on the state of the kingdom.

The Lord Chancellor says that there is much evil in the land, and that justice is corrupted. He recommends reforms without delay.

The Army Commander reports that there is unrest in the mercenary army and says that many of the more powerful citizens are resisting the authority of the Emperor.

The Treasurer and the Steward bewail the lack of money in the kingdom. There is not even enough cash to make ends meet, they say.

Comment

This scene makes use of Goethe's experiences as the minister of state in Weimar. The problems of government will be one of the most important **themes** in the second part of the play.

Mephistopheles, assuming the role of the Emperor's jester, comes forward with a suggestion. Since there is much gold and treasure under the ground, he says, and since everything under the ground and above it is the property of the monarch, the way to solve the fiscal problems of the realm is to make use of this buried money. The Devil's implication, which will be developed in further scenes, is that the Emperor ought to issue some kind of certificates entitling the holders to a certain share of the hidden gold. What Mephistopheles is suggesting, in fact, is the inauguration of a system of paper money.

There is disagreement in the court about what the Devil means, and no help is provided by a confused explanation given by the Emperor's astrologer. However, the crowd at the fringes of the court realizes that the Devil is a man who knows his way around. Finally, the Emperor calls a halt to the proceedings and announces that there will be a great carnival and masquerade to celebrate Ash Wednesday and the beginning of Lent.

Spacious Hall (lines 5065-5986)

The hall is gaily decorated for the carnival.

A herald appears to announce the festivities. Do not look for any typical German revelry involving death's heads, witches, and devils, he says. For our Emperor has been to Italy and wishes to have his carnival in the Italian manner. Gaiety and flowers and splendid colors are the order of the day.

Comment

The herald's announcement describes the difference between Part I and Part II of *Faust*. Whereas the first part was dark and gloomy, the second part will be primarily light and gay. And the reason for the difference is at least partly the one the herald ascribes to the Emperor. Between the writing of Part I and Part II Goethe had made a journey to Italy and was greatly influenced by his trip.

The spacious hall is filled with flower girls and splendidly costumed figures representing various fruits and flowers. Song and music fill the room. Then a group of young and beautiful girls enters, followed by a group of rough fishermen, hunters, and woodcutters. The two groups frolic and converse.

A band of poets then comes in to provide entertainment. However, disputes arise among them, and characters from Greek mythology replace them to present a pageant.

A great number of mythological figures make speeches and converse together. Then Plutus, the god of riches, arrives, to help the Emperor out of his financial trouble. He proves to be a very wise man. He states that joy and truth and beauty are more valuable than riches. Then he waves his magic wand and gold seems to pour from the earth. The people at the carnival close in to grab some for themselves. However, the herald drives them back and reminds them that it is only a pageant. What seems to be gold is really brass, he says, for there is no gold in the kingdom to spare.

The great god Pan arrives, bringing fire and heat with him. At the close of the scene Plutus summons cooling mist to put out the blaze.

Comment

Part II is almost twice as long as Part I. In the second part there is a great diversity of scenes and scenes-within-scenes. In many of the scenes neither Faust nor Mephistopheles appear, and there is no explanation of how they get from one place to another. The Devil, for example, arrives at the semi-legendary court of the Emperor with no enlightenment for the reader about what he is doing there, or what the Emperor has to do with the life of Faust (who is, after all, the subject of the play). It is noteworthy that Part II is almost one-fourth over at this point, and Faust and the Devil have not appeared together yet. That will come in the next scene.

Pleasure Garden (lines 5987–6172)

We are still at the Emperor's court. It is the morning after the festivities described in the preceding scene. The sun shines brightly. The Emperor enters with his retinue. Faust and Mephistopheles are part of the group.

Forgive me for my use of fire last night, Faust says. Thus we learn that the doctor was the director of the preceding pageant, although he did not appear.

That is quite all right, the Emperor replies. I thoroughly enjoyed the whole evening.

At this point the Steward and Army Commander enter in a rush. I have wonderful news, the Steward says. By something that seems almost like a miracle, our kingdom is suddenly free of debts. The army too has been paid, the commander adds. There seems to be a new spirit in the land.

The Treasurer enters and tells the Emperor to ask Faust how all this came about. Let the Lord Chancellor tell it, Faust says as the old chancellor arrives.

The Lord Chancellor is happy. He reads a certificate in his hand that is like the one Mephistopheles proposed in the second scene of the act. The certificate is signed with the Emperor's signature.

The Emperor is fearful of some kind of fraud. How did you get my signature? he asks.

The Treasurer explains that during the festival the preceding night the Emperor, dressed as the Greek god Pan, had signed a document as part of the masque. This signature had been reproduced on the certificates, he explains.

The Emperor is amazed that the people value the certificates (paper money) as much as they value gold. However, he agrees to the arrangement. He says that Faust and Mephistopheles will receive honor for their invention of the new kind of money.

Then, in his great happiness, the Emperor gives presents to all members of the court. Whatever they wish for most in life is given to them.

A Gloomy Gallery (lines 6173-6306)

Faust and Mephistopheles are alone. What brings you here to talk to me when you have the glittering court to go to? Mephistopheles asks.

The Emperor thinks I am a great magician, Faust answers, and now he demands that I make Helen of Troy and Paris stand before him. I have promised him I would and my promise must not be broken.

Mephistopheles is reluctant to fulfill Faust's wish but the doctor badgers him and finally extracts an answer from the Devil.

The way to seek departed figures of mythology is through the Mothers, Mephistopheles says. They live beneath the floor of the earth and are creatures of great mystery. Even the devils do not like to speak of them.

I have had enough of your empty-minded magic, Faust says. Can't you tell me anything without all this mystery?

If you want to see Helen and Paris you must grope in the void, the Devil replies. You must enter a realm of limitless space. For you can reach the gods in no other way.

I am not afraid, Faust retorts. I am willing to explore pure nothingness, for in that empty space the All may be found.

Then take this key, Mephistopheles says, handing it to him.

It sparkles in my hand, Faust says in wonder.

Do not be afraid, says Mephistopheles. Take the key and with it descend to the lower depths.

There you will see a tripod surrounded by the strange figures called the Mothers. There is a great peril, but walk through them to the glowing tripod that stands in the center of the crowd of spirits. Touch the tripod with the key and bring it back with you. You will have safe conduct. With the tripod you will be enabled to call heroic spirits from the deep.

How do I descend? Faust asks.

Stamp on the ground with all your might, Mephistopheles answers. Faust does so and sinks beneath the earth.

Comment

So begins another great adventure for Faust. However, we must notice how different it is from his preceding ones in the first part of the play. First of all, the influence of the Devil is much less evident. Mephistopheles is not even going to accompany him to see the Mothers, although he has shown the doctor the way. Second, the present situation has an element of unreality about it. While Gretchen was a flesh-and-blood creature living in the real world, Faust is here dealing with spirits and mythological figures. No doubt the threat to his life is as great as in Part I, but the threat to his soul does not seem so overwhelming because it is cast in an unreal setting. (For a summary of the story of Helen of Troy and Paris see the Comment on page 63.)

State Rooms (lines 6307-6376)

The Emperor and his court are gathered in a brightly lit room to see Paris and Helen of Troy, whom Faust has promised to display to the court. We learn later that Faust has been successful in his mission to the Mothers and has gotten the mythological couple.

The Chamberlain and Steward of the court ask Mephistopheles to bring on the spirit scene he and Faust promised. The Emperor is a powerful man and will not wait, they say.

My colleague has gone to take care of it, the Devil replies. The working of his deep magic arts takes time.

While the court is waiting for the completion of Faust's task, various ladies of the court, relying on Mephistopheles' reputation as a magician, ask him for various beauty secrets. He tells them of some remedies and love potions and a large group of them crowd around, seeking more advice.

I've had enough of this, Mephistopheles says in disgust. I wish Faust would be speeded on his way by the Mothers.

Then Mephistopheles sees the court leaving the State Rooms to go into the Baronial Hall, where the pageant with Helen and Paris is to be presented. He is greatly relieved to find that Faust has returned and is preparing the show.

Baronial Hall (lines 6377-6565)

The lighting is dim, as if for the showing of a play. The Emperor and his court are in their seats, waiting.

The Herald and the court Astrologer announce that the show is about to begin. Mephistopheles pops his head up from the prompter's box and says that he intends to provide eloquent comments on the proceedings. The Devil is very good at prompting, he says ironically.

By magic, a temple in the classical style appears on the stage. An architect in the audience says it does not suit his taste. The Astrologer announces that the audience will see some strange sights. Faust appears by magic and takes his place on the stage as director of the show. He dedicates the play to the Mothers.

In a burst of magic and music, Paris appears. The ladies of the court marvel at his beauty. A knight says he looks like a shepherd and not like a prince.

Paris reclines in slumber on the stage. Helen of Troy appears.

So this is the famous beauty, Mephistopheles remarks from the prompting box. I wouldn't lose any sleep over her.

The Astrologer, however, says that her beauty is beyond words. Faust agrees, and says that he worships her with the frenzy of his innermost heart. He vows to entwine his life with hers.

Comment

Faust is in love again. The next three acts will tell of his quest and conquest of the elusive Helen of Troy. The differences between this and his love for Gretchen parallel the general differences between Parts I and II. The affair in Part I was intensely dramatic and pursued from start to finish with only a few interruptions. The affair with Helen will be more relaxed and there will be frequent undramatic breaks in the action. Whereas the interludes in Part I seemed to be a relief from the high passions of the major scenes, the interludes in Part II will be much more numerous and will seem to be natural components of the play. In other words, the structure of Part II is much less tense and has room for all sorts of flights of fancy.

Be careful, Mephistopheles says to Faust after the doctor has completed his worshipful speech about Helen. You are overstepping your part in the pageant, the Devil says.

The court women make various catty remarks about Helen.

Helen goes over to the sleeping Paris and kisses him gently.

Faust does not like this, but Mephistopheles advises him to be quiet and let the story take its course.

Paris wakes up. He is amazed at the sight of the beautiful Helen. Suddenly he seizes her and begins to carry her away.

Comment

This pageant represents the first meeting of Helen and Paris at her husband's home in Sparta (also known as Lacedaemon). According to the legend, Paris raped Helen and took her away with him to Troy. Helen, however, was not reluctant to go with him. As we shall see, Faust will interrupt the recreation of this legend and prevent it from happening again.

Stop, fool! Faust shouts as Paris carries Helen away. You will rue this day. Faust breaks in on the scene and seizes Helen. He touches Paris with his magic key. There is a thunderous explosion. Faust is thrown to the ground, where he lies senseless The spirits of Helen and Paris fade away.

Mephistopheles steps forward and picks Faust up. He walks away with the doctor over his shoulder. There you have it, the Devil says as he leaves. It is best to have no dealings with fools (meaning Faust), for even the Devil can be struck by lightning.

ACT TWO

Narrow Gothic Chamber (lines 6566-6818)

The room is the same one in which we saw Faust during the first scene of the First Part of the Tragedy. The doctor's study is exactly as he left it All the books and papers and scientific instruments are in their accustomed places. (We learn later that after Faust's pact with Mephistopheles and his subsequent disappearance from his school, Wagner took over the doctor's duties. However, out of honor for his former teacher, he has left Faust's study exactly as it was.)

Mephistopheles stands over a bed on which Faust lies stretched out, still unconscious from the thunderbolt in the preceding scene.

Mephistopheles speaks. Lie there until you get over the shock Helen has brought you, he says to the senseless Faust. Then the Devil looks around the dusty room. He picks up Faust's old teaching gown and shakes it. A cloud of crickets and moths fly out. The insects sing a song of praise to the Devil.

Mephistopheles puts on the gown and summons the famulus who has taken Wagner's place. The man, named Nicodemus, is terrified at the sight of a man with blazing eyes wearing the robe of his former master.

Nicodemus and the Devil talk over old times. Now Wagner has become the learned doctor, and Faust is in the shade, Mephistopheles says. Then he asks Nicodemus to take him to see Wagner.

I hesitate to disturb him, the assistant says. He is up night and day working on some new experiment. However, Nicodemus goes out to fetch Wagner.

Mephistopheles, still wearing the gown, sits down in Faust's old chair. The same student whom he interviewed while pretending to be Faust comes through the door into the study.

The student, now a graduate (baccalaureus), says to himself that he will not easily be made a fool of again. Then, out loud, he says to the Devil: I find you just the same as before, but you will find me a much more learned man.

You must have accumulated much experience since I saw you last, the Devil says after the two have matched wits for a while.

Experience is only transitory, the baccalaureus says. The mind is the thing. Then the ex-student compares Mephistopheles' head with the skulls on the shelf of the study. Both are equally empty, he says.

Do you think that you have the right to be rude? the Devil asks.

In German, people who talk politely are liars, the baccalaureus retorts.

Comment

This remark is much quoted, usually in the form "In German only liars are polite." It is one of the many references in the play to various traits of the German language and character.

The youthful baccalaureus continues his attack on Mephistopheles, whom he considers old and over the hill. When a man is past thirty, the graduate says, he might as well throw in the towel. Only the young can fully appreciate the glories of living and of the mind. With this, the baccalaureus leaves.

The Devil is old, Mephistopheles says to the audience. If you want to understand him, you have to grow old too.

Laboratory (lines 6819-7004)

This is the room where Wagner carries on his experiments. There is fantastic scientific apparatus all over the place. Wagner is tending his furnace, over which he has a bottle simmering.

Mephistopheles enters. Quiet, Wagner says. For I am about to conclude a wonderful achievement. I am making a human being.

After some more work at the furnace, the bottle begins to glow and a tiny figure appears in it. It is Homunculus (which means, literally, small man). Homunculus calls Wagner "father" and Mephistopheles "cousin" and carries on a lively but shallow conversation with them. Then a side door opens, revealing Faust still unconscious on the bed.

Homunculus, still in the bottle, glides over to where Faust lies. Hovering over him, he tells the others that Faust is dreaming of swans and nymphs. We should take him to the Classical Walpurgis Night, the little figure says. It would suit his mood.

What is the "Classical" Walpurgis Night? Mephistopheles asks.

Homunculus, who has already indicated that he knows who Mephistopheles is, explains: You know only about Romantic ghosts. The Classical ghosts are the true ones. Your gloomy Walpurgis Night was held in the north; we have to go south for the Classical one, to the plain of the Peneus River.

Comment

This is an important comment about the two Parts of the play. As has been noted, after the First Part was written, Goethe made a trip to Italy and was influenced by its classical atmosphere. The two Walpurgis Nights, the Classical and the Romantic, illustrate the differences between Goethe's states of mind in the two Parts of the play.

Fascinated by the idea, Mephistopheles agrees to go. The two (the Devil and Homunculus) leave the disappointed Wagner behind, even though he wants to go. Of course, they take the unconscious Faust, for their purpose is to wake him at the gathering of the Classical spirits.

Before they go, Homunculus tells Wagner to go on with his dull and useless studies. You will become famous and, perhaps, will even find virtue, the little man-made man says.

When all is said and done, Mephistopheles says to the audience as the scene ends, we depend on the creatures we have made.

Comment

The Devil's comment is similar to one made by the famous German atheist Ludwig Feuerbach, who lived in the nineteenth century. Feuerbach said: "Man created God in his own image."

Classical Walpurgis Night (lines 7005-8487)

The scene is a plain in Greece. The spirits of classical antiquity have assembled for their annual gathering.

Pharsalian Fields

Homunculus and Mephistopheles arrive from the air, carrying Faust. They comment on the various spirits they see. When Faust touches the ground he awakes. His first words are: "Where is she?"

Homunculus says he does not know. However, he recommends that Faust go from spirit to spirit and ask for Helen.

Mephistopheles says that they should separate, each to seek the adventures he desires. Homunculus will bring them together again by lighting a magic lantern. They leave and Faust is alone.

This Grecian soil refreshes me, Faust says. I am ready to look for Helen again. No matter what the danger, I must find her.

On the Upper Peneus

Mephistopheles engages in conversation with griffins and sphinxes. Then Faust enters and asks the sphinxes if they have seen Helen. They tell Faust to find Chiron, who knows. Faust leaves.

Mephistopheles continues his conversation and the scene closes.

On the Lower Peneus

Nymphs and mists flutter through the scene. The Peneus River says that it feels that something terrible is about to happen. Faust approaches the river.

The nymphs sing to Faust and suggest that he lie down in the shade and rest.

Faust speaks of the beauty of the place and the wonder of the spirits hovering around it. Then Chiron enters on horseback.

Faust asks him to stop so that he can question him. Chiron says that he hasn't the time but suggests the Faust ride along with him so they can talk. Faust mounts the horse behind Chiron and they ride off.

The two riders talk of various figures from mythology. Then Faust shifts the conversation to Helen, and Chiron tells him a legend about the beautiful woman's youth. When she was ten years old she was already attractive to men, Chiron says.

The riders arrive at a battlefield where Greece and Rome once fought. At temple there, they meet Manto, the guardian, and talk with him. Manto is to take Faust down to Helen. They go down the steps together. Manto tells Faust not to be afraid.

Again on the Upper Peneus

A large number of spirits, including Seismos, the terrible creator of earthquakes, are talking with each other. Mephistopheles appears in the midst of these fantastic creatures. He is unsure of himself for he is out of his own territory.

I wish I were back at the Brocken where our Walpurgis Night is held, Mephistopheles says.

The Lamiae, a group of femmes fatales, try to lure the Devil to follow them. Mephistopheles does.

Mephistopheles tries to seize them and they turn into nothing. You do not deserve more, the Lamiae taunt.

The Devil again bewails his fate to be among strange spirits in a strange land. Then he wanders around among the rocks and discovers he is lost.

Comment

The ironic implication of this scene is that the Devil lives in Germany and does not know his way around anywhere else. In other words, Germany is the Devil's preserve-that is, it is a minor form of Hell.

At this point, Homunculus appears. Mephistopheles is glad to see him.

Homunculus tells Mephistopheles that he has been listening to the wisdom of two Greek philosophers, Thales and Anaxagoras. Mephistopheles advises him not to depend on other men's words for wisdom but rather to use his own mind.

Homunculus thanks him for the good advice and the two separate again. Homunculus returns to hear more of the argument between Thales and Anaxagoras.

The argument concerns the composition of the world. Thales believes that water is the important element. Anaxagoras holds that the earth is primarily composed of fire. The two argue as Homunculus listens, urging them on.

Comment

Thales and Anaxagoras were actual philosophers who lived before the age of Socrates, the Greek who brought reason to the practice of philosophy. While it may seem silly to us now, the pre-Socratic philosophers seriously entertained these and similar theories about the composition of the earth. They were trying to get to basic truths about man and his life on earth. Without the precise methods and empirical concepts of modern science, they were limited to considering the earth in terms of the elementary substances they knew, including air and water. They tried to find out by argument which was the primal substance from which the earth took its shape.

Finally the argument is over, although not settled to anyone's satisfaction. The philosophers disappear.

Mephistopheles climbs over the rocks and appears on the scene. He is still homesick for his "native" Germany and recalls some of the features of that country.

Phorkyas, one of the sisters known as the Phorkyads, asks who is approaching as Mephistopheles stumbles onto their temple. The Phorkyads are tremendously ugly; the Devil finds them appealing and strikes up a long conversation with them.

The sisters teach Mephistopheles how to look as ugly as they do. They tell him to squint one eye and let his teeth hang over his lip.

The Devil thanks them for the knowledge. He will use it to scare his fellow devils, Mephistopheles says.

Rockly Inlets of the Aegean: The moon hangs over the ocean. Sirens, Nereids, and Tritons, all mythical creatures of the sea, sing of the night and the water. Thales, who supported water as the primal element of the earth, appears with Homunculus.

Proteus, a figure from mythology who can change his shape at will, shows some samples of his art. Other spirits appear and they all talk.

Galatea, another sea creature, glides up in a chariot made of shell. Homunculus, the ugly little man, is amazed at her beauty. He wants to join her but instead dashes himself on her shell. The bottle protecting him is broken and he is dissolved in the sea. The Classical Walpurgis Night is over.

Comment

It is interesting to compare the Walpurgis Night of Part I with the Classical Walpurgis Night just summarized. The most obvious difference is the one already brought out by Homunculus: The one in the first part was Romantic, the one in the second part was Classical. The first one was ugly and gloomy and gruesome; and the second one has some of these elements but is primarily light and airy. The difference between the nights is the same as the difference between the climate of Greece and the climate of Germany.

ACT THREE

Menelaus' Palace In Sparta (lines 8488-9126)

Helen enters with a chorus led by Panthalis. She tells of her adventures in Troy and of her return to her homeland. Her husband, Menelaus, is celebrating the event on the beach with his army.

Comment

After Helen was taken to Troy by Paris, Menelaus and his brother, Agamemnon, led a Greek expedition to Troy to recover her. After ten years of fighting, the Greeks got inside the walls of the city by using the famous trick of the Trojan horse. Paris was killed in the war and Troy was sacked by the Greeks. Now Helen has returned with her husband to Sparta, where Menelaus is king.

    The chorus and Helen enter into a long dialogue about what is past and what is yet to come. They speak in the Greek form of poetry, which is syllabic rather than rhyming; that is, the poetic feeling is obtained by regulating the number of syllables in the line.

    After a while, Phorkyas, one of the ugly sisters Mephistopheles encountered during the Classical Walpurgis Night, appears and talks bitterly about beauty. She tells of the trouble that beautiful women have caused.

    The chorus remarks that when Phorkyas is seen with Helen, Phorkyas seems uglier than when she is seen alone.

Phorkyas then tells Helen that Menelaus plans to kill her and her maids. All are terrified and say that they do not want to die. They ask the old, ugly Phorkyas for a solution to their terrible dilemma.

Phorkyas tells them of the one possibility of escape. There is a nearby king who rules many troops, she says. He has gained much power while the Greeks were away at the Trojan war and might be willing to shelter Helen and her maids.

Helen asks questions about this king. (We learn later that the king is Faust.) Phorkyas (who, we learn later, is Mephistopheles in disguise) answers them in a vague way but tells them that if the powerful king comes there will be no reason to fear Menelaus.

Trumpets are heard in the distance. The chorus describes the approach of Faust's army. Helen and her maids leave to take refuge in Faust's castle. At first they are doubtful about their fate with the strange king, but eventually their fears diminish and they approach the castle hopefully.

Castle Courtyard (lines 9127-9573)

The scene is in the inner courtyard of a vast medieval castle. There are many towers and decorations typical of the Middle Ages, and they form a strange contrast with the Greek setting we have just left.

The chorus of her maids looks to Helen for advice on how to proceed. Helen asks to be led to the lord of the castle (Faust) even though she has not been given a welcome befitting a queen. She is tired and wants to rest, Helen says.

The maids of the chorus demand a rich throne and splendid decorations for Helen, their queen. Attendants arrive and fulfill the chorus' wishes.

At the end of the train is the lord of the castle, Faust, dressed as a medieval knight. It is a long time since Faust has appeared in the play. The last time we saw him was during the Classical Walpurgis Night, when Manto led him down the temple steps to meet Helen.

Faust approaches Helen with his watchman, Lynceus, in chains at his side.

Comment

Lynceus appears several times more in various scenes. At the very end she provides a valuable and revealing comparison with Faust. We should watch him carefully, for though he does not have much to say and is an ambiguous person, he is nevertheless important in the play.

Faust explains why he has Lynceus in chains. He was supposed to watch from the castle tower for the approach of strangers and report their movements and identity to his lord. However, he neglected to tell anyone of Helen's arrival and thus she was not given a reception befitting a queen. As an apology, Faust offers to do to Lynceus whatever Helen demands.

Helen is flattered by the attention and responsibility Faust is giving her. She asks Lynceus to explain himself.

Lynceus says that he saw Helen's approach very well. However, he says, he was so astounded by her beauty that he forgot his duty and just stared at her.

Helen cannot punish a man for admiring her beauty, so she forgives the watchman.

Faust takes the opportunity to praise Helen's beauty too. He says that he is hers.

Lynceus reappears with a long train of attendants bearing coffers of jewels and other precious things. He makes a long speech in which he heaps praises on Helen's priceless beauty.

Comment

Lynceus' speech, like his preceding one, is in **rhyme**, whereas Faust and Helen and the rest speak in the Greek poetic mode mentioned earlier. Helen is attracted to the watchman's poetry and later convinces Faust to speak in it too. At several points, when answering Faust, she provides **rhymes** for the last line of his speech. This is another example of Goethe's masterful use of poetry as a dramatic device.

Faust again joins the tribute to Helen. He pledges his allegiance to her and says that she may have anything in his kingdom that she wishes.

Helen invites Faust to take his place at the throne beside her own. After kissing her hand, Faust accepts and takes his place as coregent.

Helen tells Faust how much she likes the rhymed speech of Lynceus. The words follow one another naturally and seem to end with a caress, she says.

Faust agrees to try the rhymed poetic form and the two lovers exchange words of love in verse. The chorus, still speaking in the Greek mode, provides a background for their billing and cooing.

Suddenly, Phorkyas appears. While you are talking your lovers' talk, she says roughly to Faust and Helen, the army of Menelaus is approaching. Don't you feel the danger?

You seem to take joy in bringing bad news, Faust says. Then he turns to his army and urges them to join battle with Menelaus. The sounds of fighting are heard off-stage as Faust urges his men on.

Then Faust takes his place again beside Helen and tells her that bliss is on the way for them. By magic, Faust transforms the scene into fabled Arcadia.

Arcadia (lines 9574-10038)

All is green and peaceful. The maids of the chorus lay scattered here and there in sleep.

Phorkyas enters and wakes the chorus. I have something to tell you, she says. She then relates to them what is going on between Helen and Faust. The lovers are secluded in a bower, she says, and are gasping with affection for each other.

The chorus is skeptical of Phorkyas' strange tale, but they allow her to continue.

Phorkyas then tells them that a wondrous son has been born to Faust and Helen. The boy is beautiful and active and takes great joy in life. He is the future master of all beauty, a sweet and eternal music seems to permeate him. He is a child of rapture.

Exquisite, pure music is heard coming from the cave where Faust and Helen and their son live. That kind of music could only come from an overflowing heart, Phorkyas says.

Helen, Faust, and their child, named Euphorion, emerge from the cave. Euphorion tells his parents that his presence should make them ever closer in their love. Faust and Helen, in a series of interlocked poems, agree with their son.

I must be leaping and springing through the air, Euphorion sings. These thoughts of joy and flight are uppermost in my mind. I don't want to be earthbound any longer.

Comment

According to many commentators, Euphorion represents the spirit of romantic poetry. Like Goethe and his youthful poetry, Euphorion wants to experience great passion and a soaring away from the earth into some ideal realm of pure beauty. Lord Byron, the English romantic poet of the nineteenth century, whom Goethe greatly admired, may have served as the model for the spirit of Euphorion and the spirit of romantic poetry. Byron too was interested in wild adventures and high passions, and he too died young, while fighting with a band of romantic revolutionaries in Greece.

Faust and Helen ask their son to curb his soaring desires. Euphorion agrees and leads the chorus of maids in a graceful dance. Then the group sings a lovely song.

However, Euphorion's high spirits are not to be contained for long and he begins a wild chase with the girls in an attempt to embrace them. You are the quarry and I am the hunter, he says to them. The pursuer and the pursued run off.

What mad passion, what wild riot, Faust and Helen say. There is no hope of sweet restraint.

The chorus re-enters. Euphorion follows, bearing a young girl. The youth embraces the unwilling girl and kisses her passionately. The girl bursts into flame and soars into the sky. Follow me into space and among the deep crags, the flaming spirit cries back to Euphorion.

The boy climbs up the cliffs in a frenzy of joy and longing. I must get higher and survey the whole wide world, he calls back.

The chorus tries to convince him that a peaceful life is best, but Euphorion answers that it was not meant for him.

Helen and Faust call up to him. You have barely entered the morning of your life and yet you yearn for the ultimate heights, they say. You are too rash.

Euphorion calls back that he is not afraid of danger. Danger is a part of a man's life if he wishes to reach his goal, the youth exclaims.

Then his striving for the heights reaches its peak and he casts himself from the cliff into the air. For a moment, held up by the air, Euphorion remains suspended as if by a miracle. Then the illusion shatters and he falls crashing at his parents' feet. His body fades away; only his clothes and his lyre are left on the earth.

Helen and Faust bemoan their loss. Our joys are brief, they say; woes overwhelm us.

The voice of Euphorion rises from the deep. Mother, it calls, do not forsake me!

The chorus sings a lament for the departed youth, saying that poetry will always rise aspiring from the earth.

Helen makes her last, sad speech to Faust. The ancient prophecy is fulfilled, she says. Happiness and beauty cannot be joined long in the same body. I must say farewell, for both life and love are gone. Helen of Troy embraces Faust and her body vanishes. Her silken robes are left in the doctor's hands.

Hold fast to the robes, Phorkyas says to the bereaved Faust. They will carry you away. We will meet again at a distant place.

Helen's robes dissolve into clouds, which envelop Faust. He is borne aloft and disappears from the scene.

As the curtain falls at the end of the act Phorkyas takes off her mask to reveal that she is really Mephistopheles.

Comment

Thus ends Faust's love affair with Helen of Troy. Outwardly, his affair with Gretchen ended in a similar way. Both endings were tragic and sad. However, Faust's parting with Gretchen was drawn out and almost unbearable in its pathos and intensity, while his separation from Helen is sudden and almost light. He does not even have a chance to say anything about Helen's disappearance. But in Part I, he berated himself time and again as the inevitability of Gretchen's tragic end, and his responsibility for it, became apparent. This again demonstrates the romantic qualities of the first part of the tragedy and the classical aspects of the second part.

ACT FOUR

Mountain Heights (lines 10039-10344)

The scene is a mighty peak strewn with jagged rocks. A cloud draws near the summit and settles on an overhanging ledge. The cloud is dispelled and Faust steps forward.

Faust delivers a soliloquy on the strange method of his arrival and the solitude of his surroundings. He sees a vision of a beautiful woman in the clouds and wonders if it signifies a return to the bliss of his youth.

A seven-league boot crosses the stage, followed by another. Mephistopheles alights and the boots stride away.

That's what I call traveling in style, the Devil says. But what made you choose this desolate place? he asks Faust. It used to be part of the floor of Hell.

Mephistopheles then tells the story of the creation of the mountains. The forces of Hell were too powerful for the earth's crust, he says, so the crust blew up and parts of Hell were thrown up as mountain crags and peaks.

Faust does not believe the Devil. The doctor says that nature was too perfect in its creation to use any part of Hell. However, he says, it is interesting to look at nature from the Devil's angle.

Then Faust reveals to Mephistopheles that he has formed a great plan about how to spend the rest of his days. He asks the Devil to guess what it is.

The Devil suggests several things, including the building of a pleasure palace that would contain everything a man might desire. There would be plenty of girls to fulfill Faust's desires, the Devil says, for he has always preferred women in the plural for sport.

That is old hat, Faust says, rejecting Mephistopheles' conjectures.

Comment

Faust has come a long way since we met him in despair in the First Part of the Tragedy. Then he was ready to try anything to gain pleasure, and said specifically that he wanted to indulge in all the excesses known to devotees of the Devil. However, we have found Faust surprisingly modest in his demands. He has asked for and received love affairs with Gretchen and Helen, and he had worldly power. However, he has indulged in none of the excesses he dreamed about in his earlier days. Now we find Faust on the verge of a surprising decision that marks the beginning of his redemption, for he is about to undertake a project that requires work and is meant to be for the good of mankind.

Faust tells Mephistopheles what he wants: he would like to gain control of a strip of coastline on the sea and reclaim the land by building a series of dikes. In this battle against the tides and the oceans he feels he will find what he has been searching for everywhere.

In an aside, Mephistopheles says that he knew Faust would ask for this all along.

Then a sound of drums and parade music is heard off stage.

If you want to get the land for your project, here is a good way to do it, Mephistopheles says. For our friend the Emperor is about to go to war. If we help him win he will give us the coastal strip as a reward.

Faust and Mephistopheles cross to another mountain and view the positions of the opposing armies in the plain below. We can win easily with a little help, the Devil says. Then he summons forth the Three Mighty Men to help him and Faust. He appoints the doctor commander-in-chief of the army.

The Three Mighty Men, Faust, and Mephistopheles go off together to fight the battle.

Mountain Foothills (lines 10345–10782)

The Emperor and his military aides discuss the situation. It seems that a rival emperor is trying to gain control of the Emperor's throne and the battle will decide who will sit in the contested seat.

Faust appears and offers the Emperor the use of his friends and his magic in the Emperor's cause. The emperor gladly accepts, and turns over the command of his forces to Faust.

With the help of the Three Mighty Men and some magic from Mephistopheles that disturbs the enemy army, Faust's forces win the day.

Rival Emperor's Tent (lines 10783-11042)

Faust's victorious troops, including one of the Three Mighty Men, are attempting to carry off large bags of gold from the tent of the Emperor's defeated rival.

The Emperor enters the scene, proclaiming the victory of his forces. He begins to distribute rewards to the lords who have helped him in the campaign. One of the lords present is an Archbishop.

The Archbishop, in a bitter exchange with the Emperor, recalls some of the Emperor's past sins and by a kind of spiritual blackmail extorts some gifts of land from the monarch. Even then, though, the Archbishop is not satisfied. He says he has heard that the Emperor made a gift of some shoreland to "that wicked man" Faust and says that the monarch will not be forgiven for this latest sin unless the revenues from the land are given to the Church.

The Emperor, very disgusted by this time, tells the greedy Archbishop that there can be no revenues from the land as it is still under water.

The Archbishop replies that someday the land will be reclaimed and that the Church expects to get its share when that time comes.

Comment

The scene between the Archbishop and the Emperor shows Goethe's low opinion of the Catholic Church. Although Faust has a religious **theme**, it is not a **theme** that is dependent on the teachings of any church for its significance. Goethe's religion implies a personal bond between man and God; no intermediary is necessary in this almost pantheistic system. Thus, Goethe rejects the organized Church. Some critics have felt that the outcome of the play depends upon a particular Catholic or Protestant theology. Actually, as the preceding scene has shown, Goethe is a free thinker who believes that a man's reason is sufficient to create his own theology.

ACT FIVE

Open Country (lines 11043–11142)

A Wanderer appears. He is revisiting the scenes of his childhood and sees a simple cottage beneath the linden trees that he once knew well. The occupants of the cottage, an old man and his wife, helped him in earlier days.

Baucis, the old woman, and Philemon, the old man, tell the Wanderer what has happened during the years he has been away. Faust has turned formerly barren land at the edge of the sea into blooming gardens and fields. But the aged Faust is still not satisfied; he wants Baucis and Philemon's cottage, which is the only piece of property in the area that he does not own. The old couple admits that he has offered them another estate in return for theirs, but they do not want to give up their old home.

As the sun goes down, Baucis and Philemon make their way to the chapel to pray.

Palace (lines 11143-11287)

The scene is an ornamental garden in Faust's palace. Faust, very old, is walking in the garden and thinking.

Comment

Although Faust's exact age at this time is not given in the play, we know from a statement of Goethe's that has come down to us that the doctor is supposed to be 100 years old.

Lynceus, the watchman whom we met in the Helen of Troy **episode**, sings a beautiful little song about the ships approaching the harbor as the sun sets.

Faust is walking in the garden, brooding about his failure to acquire the land of Philemon and Baucis.

Mephistopheles and the Three Mighty Men get off the boats, which have just arrived with a rich cargo. They tell Faust that their trading and pirating voyage was successful; they left with two ships and have come back with twenty.

Faust asks the Devil and the Three Mighty Men to get the aged couple Philemon and Baucis out of the way and to acquire their property for him.

Deep Night (Lines 11288-11383)

Lynceus, the watchman, tells of his philosophy of life. All bright things pleased him in his life if they lasted, he says, but most of all he found delight in himself.

Comment

Compare this simple statement about the joys of life with the complaints of Faust in Part I, when he said nothing on the earth could please him. Lynceus makes a telling answer to Faust's despair: Have faith in yourself and you will find happiness.

Lynceus' reverie is disturbed when he sees a fire at the old couple's cottage under the linden trees.

Faust is musing about his latest acquisition of land. He believes that the old couple has been transferred to another estate.

Mephistopheles enters with the Three Mighty Men and tells Faust that the old couple is dead. Faust is upset, for he had given instructions not to kill them but merely to transfer them to another home. Mephistopheles and his henchmen leave.

Faust, standing alone on the castle balcony, feels a premonition of death.

Midnight (lines 11384-11510)

A spirit in the form of Care enters Faust's room.

Faust tells Care what he has learned from all his adventures. Man should worry about only what is possible in life, and not seek after infinity and the eternal. Thus, a man may wander through life from day to day. In his wanderings he will find both joy and agony, but at least he will not be plagued by ghosts.

Care says that there is no restfulness in life. Faust says he has been through all this before and asks the ghost to leave. Instead, Care blinds Faust. A human being is blind all his life and that is how you shall meet your end, Faust, Care says as she leaves.

Outer Court Of Palace (lines 11511-11603)

Mephistopheles is overseeing some land reclamation work being carried out by a band of lemurs. Faust, blinded, gropes his way forward. How the clanking of the shovels makes me happy, he says. Then he advises Mephistopheles about how to carry on the work.

I am giving you the highest wisdom I have, Faust says. This is the best that man can hope to know. Practical knowledge put to use in an active life is man's joy and happiness. If I could be among men who lead such lives then I might say to the moment: "Stay, you are so fair." This is the great moment of my life.

Faust sinks backward and dies.

Comment

Thus ends the mortal life of Dr. Heinrich Faust. The lesson he has learned is a simple one. Man should not try to be like a god but rather should try to be like a man. He should not strive to know everything and experience every pleasure but instead should be satisfied with his lot, though still striving to improve it within the bounds of his capabilities.

Mephistopheles is disgusted that Faust has died, for the Devil has not been able to trick the doctor into saying he was supremely happy before his time was up. However, the Devil is confident that he will regain possession of Faust's soul.

Burial Scene: (lines 11604-11844)

The lemurs are burying Faust. Mephistopheles waits with his companions from Hell to take possession of the soul of the deceased.

Suddenly the air is filled with the singing of angels. They descend on the scene, strewing rose petals. For a moment they distract Mephistopheles and his men with their beauty. In this moment, the angels take Faust's soul and fly away with it.

Mephistopheles is defeated, for he has lost the soul of Faust. He berates himself for his bungling and for the waste of his investment. But he admits that he was tricked for a moment when the angels came into a feeling that was close to love. He was beaten, the Devil admits, but the forces that overwhelmed him were not small ones.

> Comment

This is the last we see of Mephistopheles. He bows out gracefully.

Mountain Gorges (lines 11844-12110)

This is the last scene of the play. Forest, rocks, and desert are spread out before us. Groups of holy men are scattered on the mountainside.

The holy men sing songs in praise of the eternal and of Heaven. The angels float past, carrying the immortal part of Faust. They sing a song saying that the crowd of Heaven is coming to meet Faust's soul.

Various other choirs and holy men sing. They are joined later by the voices of women who have sinned and yet attained heaven because of their faith.

One of the singers is Una Poenitentium, formerly called Gretchen. She is ecstatic. The man whom I loved in pain has now come back to me as a pure soul, she says.

A mystical chorus concludes the play. "All things transitory are merely parables," they sing. "The insufficiency of the earth finds fulfillment in the plentitude of Heaven. In Heaven the things that cannot be expressed on earth are done through love. Eternal Womanhood leads us on to perfection."

Comment

Thus ends the Second Part of the Tragedy of *Faust*. Faust, like Gretchen, is saved and Mephistopheles is defeated. The spirit that has made it all possible, according to the final chorus, is the love of Eternal Womanhood. There is great dispute about what Goethe meant by that phrase. It is probably close to the truth to say that he was referring to the passive principle of creation in mankind, the part of man that does not strive for anything beyond itself yet still creates beauty and joy and love.

FAUST

CHARACTER ANALYSES

FAUST

Romantic

Faust is the archetypal romantic. Mephistopheles and the Lord designate him as such in the Prologue, in their dispute over the nature and goodness of man. When the Lord introduces Faust's name into the conversation, Mephistopheles comments that Faust is a man who "demands from Heaven its fairest star" and at the same time demands "from earth the highest joy it bears." In his comment Mephistopheles has focused on a paradox which identifies the romantic and which gives tension to all romantic writing. Stated simply the paradox consists of man's conflicting desires which pull him toward heaven and earth at one and the same time. This tension-with its implication of a striving for absolutes-is the source of Faust's other identifying characteristics.

Pride

In the play's opening speech, Faust proclaims his hope of discovering the secret of creation and world order. In effect, he is succumbing to what the Greeks called hubris, the desire to transcend human limitations and assume the functions of the gods. A Christian analogue of the same sin can be seen in Milton's *Paradise Lost* when Satan beguiles Eve with the promise that if she eats the apple, she will "be as the gods, / Knowing both good and evil as they know." This pride, grounded in Faust's desire to have Heaven's "fairest star," appears throughout the play, and is one of Faust's essential characteristics. When he opens his book of magic, Faust wonders if perhaps he is "a god," and shortly thereafter he refuses to yield to the spirit which appears, on the grounds that he is its equal: "Shall I yield, thing of flame, to thee?/ Faust, and thine equal I am he!"

The Importance Of The Heart

In his first conversation with Wagner - on public speaking - Faust issues a romantic manifesto in response to Wagner's question regarding the art of persuasion. Faust stresses the importance of honestly expressed feeling: "But that which issues from the heart alone, / Will bend the hearts of others to your own." He thus proclaims a typical romantic position; it is not through intellectual effort that man will move or change his fellow man, but through sincere feeling. Faust here is giving the same emphasis to the heart that Rousseau did at the beginning of the *Confessions* when he cried, "Myself alone I know the feelings of my heart," or that Wordsworth did in *The Tables Turned* with his "Come forth, and bring with you a heart / That watches and receives," Midway through the first act Faust exclaims to Mephistopheles that his end in life is not to know joy but to know in his "heart's core all human weal and woe...."

Awareness Of Limitations

A third romantic characteristic, and one which Faust continually exhibits, is the awareness that man is a dependent creature. This awareness, coupled with the desire for a spiritual absolute, causes Faust's emotional turmoil and states of depression. At one moment he wonders if he is a god; at the next he exclaims "I am not like the gods! Feel it I must;/I'm like the earth-worm, writhing in the dust...." It is Faust's dissatisfaction with the limitations of human reason which makes him turn to magic at the very beginning of the play: "I have, alas! Philosophy,/Medicine, Jurisprudence too,/and to my cost Theology,/With ardent labor, studied through./And here I stand, with all my lore,/Poor fool, no wiser than before."

Attraction Of The Abyss

The sudden depression which Faust feels at the thought that he is not a god leads him to contemplate suicide. He is here evidencing another characteristic which identifies the romantic sensibility-the strong attraction to death. Death provides an absolute and final release from the cares associated with human limitation. "I have been half in love with easeful Death" wrote Keats in *Ode to a Nightingale*, and Faust, like Keats, is half in love with death; it is a soothing escape from a life of frustration and woe. The phial of poison attracts him as though it were a "magnet" to "his sight," and he contemplates it with a sense of release: "I gaze on thee, my pain is lull'd to rest;/I grasp thee, calm'd the tumult in my breast...." But death is more than simply an escape from pain and emotional tumult-it is a test of man's godliness. Faust makes this clear when he speaks of man's ability to look into the abyss of death without shuddering as proof that man can feel the "calm sublimity of gods."

Love Of Fellow Man

Faust, like most romantics-Wordsworth and Shelley, for instance-has a strong love of his fellow man. In his opening speech he announces that part of his motivation for turning to magic is to find a "means to improve or convert mankind." Later, he exults in his humanity while walking among the village people who are in the midst of their Easter celebration: "Here am I man, I feel it here." Immediately after this, Faust willingly accepts a communion drink from one of the peasants characterized by Wagner as the "vulgar throng." Finally, at the end of the play, he dedicates himself to mankind, thereby preparing the way for his ultimate redemption.

Conscience

The Lord introduces the **theme** of conscience in his discussion with Mephistopheles at the play's beginning. Speaking of Faust, the Lord says, "A good man, even in his darkest longings,/Is well aware of the right way." Faust is essentially a good man, and this statement prepares the reader for Faust's redemption. However, it also foreshadows the Faust overtaken by his darkest longings. The scene in Margaret's bedchamber finds Faust at the height of a full-blown sensuality, but even at this point his conscience disturbs him: "And thou! ah here what seekest thou?/How quails mine inmost being now!/What wouldst thou here? what makes thy heart so sore?/Unhappy Faust! I know thee now no more." Faust's recriminations prove the Lord's statement that a good man is always "aware of the right way."

Love Of Nature

Faust's deep love of nature's beauty becomes apparent in his second conversation with Wagner. He luxuriates in the "calm beauty" of sunset and expresses a desire for wings which would enable him to soar above the earth and completely encompass the beauty of a world transformed by the setting sun. "Then should I see the world below," says Faust, "Bathed in the deathless evening-beams,/The vales reposing, every height a-glow,/The silver brooklets, meeting golden streams,/The savage mountain, with its cavern'd side,/Bars not my godlike progress." Again, toward the end of Part I, Mephistopheles and Faust discuss the value of nature in a manner which anticipates Wordsworth. When Mephistopheles chides him for wasting his time among "rocky hollows" and "caverns drear," Faust replies that contact with nature brings "new life-power." Faust's point about nature is echoed in Wordsworth's *Tintern Abbey* when the speaker praises nature as a power which ... can so inform The mind that is within us, so impress With quietness and beauty, and so feed With lofty thoughts, that neither evil tongues, Rash judgments, nor the sneers of selfish men, Nor greetings where no kindness is, nor all The dreary intercourse of daily life, Shall e'er prevail against us, or disturb Our cheerful faith, that all which we behold Is full of blessings.

What both Faust and Later Wordsworth emphasize is nature's power to sustain and regenerate man.

Attitude Toward God

It is Margaret who, in the scene in Martha's garden, elicits from Faust his conception of God. Margaret, a Christian, has begun to suspect that Faust is not a religious man, and here questions him point-blank: "Dost thou believe in God?" Faust's answer is evasive and somewhat ambiguous, but he finally indicates that he believes in an absolute. "Call it Bliss! Heart! Love! God!" Faust declares, "I have no name for it!/'Tis feeling all." His position is not traditionally Christian, but romantic. He identifies God with a feeling of absolute perfection or beauty.

WAGNER

Contrast

Faust's disciple presents a dramatic contrast to his master; he is the antithesis of everything romantic. Instead of trusting to the power of feeling and the heart, he places his faith in man's intellect. In the opening speech Faust declares his disgust with the intellect and intellectual knowledge. Wagner, however, as he demonstrates in his first conversation with Faust, is still dedicated to books and book knowledge. He, for instance believes that knowledge of rhetoric will enable him to persuade people to accept his point of view; Faust insists on the need of speaking what one honestly feels. Despite Faust's eloquence, Wagner continually misses the point of his remarks and leaves, declaring: "I have pursued my studies with diligence, and I know quite a bit, but I would like to know everything."

Mankind

Unlike Faust, Wagner abhors the common man. In the second conversation which Wagner has with Faust, he makes clear that he has nothing but loathing for the general run of humanity. He attempts to dissuade Faust from joining a crowd of people by criticizing their coarseness. "I hate the tumult of the vulgar throng," he continues, "They roar as by the evil one possess'd, / And call it pleasure, call it song."

Nature

Toward the end of their second conversation, Faust expresses his joy in the presence of nature. Wagner is unable to understand Faust's feelings; he comments that although he has had strange thoughts, he has never experienced an "impulse" such as the one witnessed in Faust. He continues, to say that nature cannot engage man's attention for long since woods and fields shrink beside the "pleasures of the mind" to be had from books.

MARGARET (GRETCHEN)

Beauty And Goodness

Margaret embodies feminine beauty and moral goodness. Mephistopheles is upset when he discovers Faust's intention to pursue her, and in his attempt to dissuade Faust he characterizes the girl. He comments on the innocence of her "virgin soul" and the fact that she is free from all sin. She is, Mephistopheles concludes, free from his control.

Ideal Love

The first song that Margaret sings reveals her strong faith in idealistic love. The song concerns a king in Thule who remained faithful to his wife's memory. A gold cup, which was the symbol of his love, could not be used without eliciting tears, and at his own death the cup was consigned to the depths of the sea. Margaret's apparent fondness for the song suggests that she too expects from love intense feeling and eternal faithfulness.

Compassion

Margaret reveals her compassionate nature in the conversation about her past life. Here, she tells Faust of her fondness for her dead sister, and describes her willing care of the child in spite of the hard work entailed.

Religion

A deep religious feeling is attributed to Margaret from the time she is introduced. Mephistopheles alludes to it with anxiety; later she gives clear evidence of it when she questions Faust about his belief. She refuses to accept his definition of God, expressing fear that he is not a Christian. Finally, she tells him that she abhors Mephistopheles, whose presence chills her blood. At the end of Part I, she refuses Faust's appeal to escape from prison and join him, since she has already given her soul to God for judgment.

MARTHA

Contrast

Martha presents the same kind of contrast to Margaret that Wagner does to Faust. Unlike Margaret, she is completely pragmatic in her approach to love. Mephistopheles is able to gain entrance to her home because she is anxious to find a new husband. It is his promise to provide a second witness to her first husband's death that persuades her to help make possible the meeting between Faust and Margaret. Mephistopheles later characterizes her when he tells Faust that she seemed made to be a procurer.

MEPHISTOPHELES

The Cynic

Mephistopheles is the archetypal cynic. In his very first speech his cynicism about the nature and goodness of man sets the stage for Faust and his conflicts. He ridicules man's intellect by suggesting that mankind would have been happier if God had not bestowed upon it a paltry reason. As things are, Mephistopheles continues, man's limited reason simply enables him to be more bestial than the beasts. Mephistopheles here expresses his opinion that man is incapable of attaining any kind of spiritual or moral perfection. He compares man to a grasshopper, and tells the Lord that He should allow man to wallow in his dung heap.

Sense Of Irony

Mephistopheles has a highly developed ironic sense. This sense of irony is exemplified in the scene in which Mephistopheles dons Faust's long robe and pretends to be the scholar while giving advice to a young student. Under the pretense of giving advice, Mephistopheles mocks logic, metaphysics, jurisprudence, and theology. His ironic sense first appears in the Prologue when he gives the impression that the only thing that separates him from the Lord is his lower-class status. "Thou seest me here once more among thy household," he says, somewhat like a black sheep returning home: "You will excuse me if I do not talk/In the high style which they think fashionable."

FAUST

CRITICAL COMMENTARY

SCOPE

To attempt a summary of critical statements dealing with Goethe's works, or even with Faust itself, would be a monumental task. Works on Goethe number in the thousands, and a thorough survey of the criticism would constitute a lifetime's work. Some attempt can be made here, however, to give a brief idea of the more significant evaluations of Faust, for the work has inspired strong feelings in critics from the nineteenth century till the present day.

BERGSTRAESSER

Arnold Bergstraesser, one of Goethe's most significant critics and biographers, calls Goethe's literary works "an image of man and society." This is a commonly accepted idea, stemming from Goethe's attempts to deal with religious, social, and **metaphysical** problems in his writing. In *Faust* he took up universal concerns: the fear of aging, disillusionment with work, the difficulty of gaining real knowledge of God, the search for absolute goodness and purity. Bergstraesser considers Goethe's primary gift to have been a philosophical one, though he also praises the man's poetic genius. He credits Goethe with the ability to "overcome despair and grow firm in the conviction that a meaningful way of life is possible, that it is worthwhile to search for truth, that beauty is real, and that good can be distinguished from evil."

THE CLASSICAL AND THE CHRISTIAN

Bergstraesser also discusses Goethe's ability to synthesize Christian and Greek ideas and traditions in his writing. Goethe is able to do this, the critic says, because he concentrated on his characters in their entire humanity, rather than as manifestations of the ideas of any particular age. This too is an evaluation which has been adopted by almost all of Goethe's critics. He transcended the labels Classical, Christian, or Romantic; rather than limit himself to one of these modes, he unified them for a many-dimensioned picture of man.

LEWISOHN

Ludwig Lewisohn, another biographer-critic, feels that Goethe was essentially a man of modern times because of the problems he investigated in *Faust*. Lewisohn, like Bergstraesser, considers Goethe to be significant because of his philosophy, but he links him to this age rather than to an earlier one. "His experiences are intensely within our own; his passions are ours, his perplexities, his anguish, his triumph."

HAMM

Victor M. Hamm in his *Patterns of Criticism* links Goethe to both the Romantic and the Classical Movement. Tracing the historical growth of the Romantic Movement, he mentions Goethe's early dislike of "romantic" ideas and his fondness for the classical ideals of strength and freshness. Hamm, like other critics, pays tribute to Goethe's ability to combine both approaches in Faust.

KAUFMANN

Walter Kaufmann, in his very significant introduction to his translation of Faust, also considers Goethe as a man who transcends the Romantic Movement: "Goethe realized the limitations of romanticism and its questionable character even before it had become the style of an age." Instead of assuming that only the highly romantic Faust speaks the poet's ideas, Kaufmann believes that Goethe spoke through Mephistopheles also. And if Faust and Mephistopheles are considered together, with the cynically realistic Mephistopheles balancing Faust's romanticism, Goethe's expression is seen to be much fuller and more controlled than it is when only the romantic ideas are taken seriously. Kaufmann, like Lewisohn, would classify Goethe as a man whose philosophy can easily be applied to modern times.

ABRAMS

M. H. Abrams, in The Mirror and the Lamp, treats Goethe's importance to the working out of an organic theory of art. He considers Goethe "distinctive" among creative writers of his time because of his interest in science (particularly biology) as well as the arts. He quotes Goethe's notes on plant metamorphosis and describes his ideas of explaining a work of art as a growing organism, like an egg or a plat. This idea of a work of art as a growing thing, unrestricted by form, was an important shaping factor during the entire Romantic Movement, and Goethe's contributions to the idea, according to Abrams, mark him as one of the great literary theoreticians as well as one of the great creative artists.

WELLEK

Rene Wellek, a prominent critic and historian of aesthetics, is quite as enthusiastic about Goethe's works as are Lewisohn and Bergstraesser. In Concepts of Criticism he qualifies the idea of Goethe the philosopher and stresses his lyrical ability, viewing him primarily as a romantic writer. "All the artistic power of Goethe is in the lyrics, in Faust ... where there is scarcely any trace of Classicism," Wellek states. He believes that Goethe's chief contributions lie in symbol, myth, and allegory, as well as in the development of the lyric voice.

CONCLUSION

Obviously, not all critics will agree with the German Hermann Grimm that Goethe was "the greatest poet" of his own time and place, or any time and any place. Many student texts, for example, carry the warning that *Faust* will be difficult reading, not to be digested the first time through. Faust especially has been criticized for structural faults, for inconsistent characterization, for concentrating too much on philosophical ideas. The facts remain, however, that the play has been read for pleasure and studied in schools for more than a hundred years; that Goethe is considered one of the significant shapers of the Romantic Movement; and that *Faust*, and the rest of his writings, are landmarks of world literature.

FAUST

ESSAY QUESTIONS AND ANSWERS

Question: Compare Part I of *Faust* with Part II.

Answer: The most obvious point of difference is that Part I is primarily romantic (passionate, emotional) and Part II is primarily classical (restrained, ordered). The first part is concerned primarily with real people, while the second part is concerned mainly with mythological figures. Part I contains more tragic elements than Part II, which is more restrained and philosophical. Moreover, the structure of Part I is more dramatic than the meandering form of Part II. This formless quality of sections of Part II makes it difficult or impossible to perform.

Question: Discuss the difference in Faust's and Wagner's attitudes toward learning and knowledge.

Answer: Faust's idea of learning (at least at the beginning of the play) is similar to that of the Renaissance man. He believes that man is capable of doing anything his mind can imagine and thus should constantly strive to overreach himself. If man wants knowledge he should seek in new places and not go back over the same ground that thousands of scholars before him have already covered. This attitude of Faust's makes him an exemplar of the traditional Renaissance view of man and of learning; it is also very much in the romantic tradition.

Wagner, on the other hand, has a medieval view of learning. He believes that knowledge comes merely from reading books and remembering what was said in them. In short, according to Faust's view man must be an adventurer and an explorer if he is to consider himself learned; Wagner believes that the learned man is merely a collector and retainer of facts and opinions.

Question: Trace the development of Faust's character and ideas through the course of the play.

Answer: When we first meet Faust he is in despair. He has studied everything in order to attain the kind of knowledge he wants, but still finds himself as ignorant as when he began. His life is dull and dusty and without joy. He has neither fame, nor fortune, nor contentment.

Then a great change comes in the life of the learned doctor. He signs a pact with the Devil in an attempt to achieve the perfection that he has for so long been seeking. However, although he tastes experience through a great many adventures, he does not find what he is seeking until the last act.

Faust finally realizes, just before he dies, that man's life, and the source of his happiness, is to live within his capabilities and put himself at the mercy of a supreme God. Man can never be completely happy but he can achieve contentment by applying himself to meaningful tasks. This is the lesson that Faust learns, just before he dies, and it represents the final development of his character.

Question: Explain the significance of the Prologue in Heaven.

Answer: The Prologue in Heaven, through the speeches of the archangels, tells us what the angels' view of knowledge and happiness is. In a less refined form, it is the view that Faust will adopt at the end of his life. Through the words of the Lord, the Prologue also gives us a hint of the eventual outcome of the drama (Faust's salvation), and thus allows us to put events in perspective as the play progresses.

Question: What are some of the artistic difficulties presented by the play as a work of art?

Answer: It is universally accepted that *Faust* is not a flawless work of art. It has been called impossible to produce at all; the characterization has been called inconsistent; and, especially in Part II, it has been criticized for lack of form.

All these criticisms are valid. What stands out, however, are not the flaws, but the overwhelming beauty of the poetry, the depth of psychological insight, the universality of the problems considered. Although it is formless in sections, and certainly has not been produced in its entirety more than a few times since its completion, it is still a powerful drama, and has, with alterations, been successfully produced for more than 100 years.

Question: In what respects can Faust be considered a representative romantic hero?

Answer: Although the play *Faust* is a combination of classical, romantic and other characteristics, its main character is in a very real sense a typical romantic hero. His personality exhibits the struggle between love of the real and the ideal worlds; he is proud of his humanity and sees himself (at first) as wholly self-sufficient; he is fascinated and tempted by the idea of death. Faust also has faith in the heart and the emotional nature of man and a deep love of humanity, as well as a love of the simple and uncomplicated world of nature.

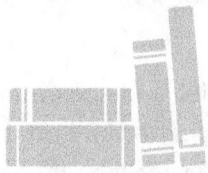

BIBLIOGRAPHY

TRANSLATIONS

Goethe, Johann Wolfgang von. *Faust.* Trans. Walter Kaufmann. New York City, 1962. Perhaps the best translation. Contains all of Part I, sections of Part II, valuable introduction by the translator.

____.*Faust.* Trans. Louis Macniece. London, 1951. Good abridged edition.

____.*Faust.* Trans. Bayard Quincy Morgan. New York, 1962. Most modern prose translation.

____.*Faust.* Trans. Bayard Taylor. New York, 1879. Good translation; the best-known version, but old now.

____.*Faust.* Erich Trunz, ed. Hamburg, Germany, 1963. Newest and most exhaustive German edition of the play.

____.*Faust.* Trans. Philip Wayne. 2 vols. New York, London, 1962. Good translation of entire play.

BACKGROUND AND CRITICAL WORKS

Abrams, M. H. *The Mirror and the Lamp.* New York, 1958. Excellent esthetic background of romanticism; essential for a real understanding of that term.

Ancelet-Hustache, Jeanne. *Goethe.* Trans. Cecily Hastings. New York 1960. Good biography with some criticism; paperback edition.

Babbitt, Irving. *Rousseau and Romanticism.* New York, 1955. Excellent attack on romanticism by a member of the group of Harvard professors involved in a re-evaluation of romantic literature. Necessary for a real understanding of its flaws and its good points.

Bergstraesser, Arnold. *Goethe's Image of Man and Society*, Chicago, 1949. Looks at Goethe and his works from a sociological and esthetic perspective.

Bernbaum, Ernest. *Guide Through the Romantic Movement.* 2nd ed. New York, 1949. Scholarly, thorough, and readable investigation of the background of romanticism from a historical and philosophical perspective.

Biermann, Berthold, ed. *Goethe's World.* New York, 1949. Gives an idea of the man and his surroundings with excerpts from letter, diaries, etc.

Cassirer, Ernest. *Rousseau, Kant, Goethe.* New York, 1945. Excellent philosophical investigation of the thought of three major romantic figures.

Fairley, Barker. *A Study of Goethe.* London, 1947. Excellent criticism of the man and the major works.

____. *Goethe as Revealed in His Poetry.* London, 1932. Esthetic evaluation of the poet and his poetry.

____. *Goethe's* Faust: *Six Essays*. London, 1953. Excellent and helpful criticism of the play.

Gillies, Alexander. *Goethe's* Faust. 1957. Excellent recent interpretation of the play; extremely helpful.

Goethe, Johann Wolfgang von. *Poetry and Truth From My Own Life*. Trans. R. O. Moon. Goethe's autobiography; immensely readable, and helpful to the student of Goethe or romanticism in general.

Hamm, Victor M. *The Pattern of Criticism*. Milwaukee, 1951. Thorough and penetrating analysis of the presuppositions behind all the major literary schools, including romanticism. Excellent background.

Hiller, Erich. *The Disinherited Mind*. New York, 1959. Philosophical work treating the major thinkers of German romanticism, including Goethe, Nietzsche, Rilke, and others.

Hulme, T. E. *Speculations*. Herbert Read, ed. New York, 1924. An excellent attack on romanticism; a standard work on the subject.

Lewisohn, Ludwig. *Goethe: The Story of a Man*. New York, 1949. Biography of the man in the words of himself and his contemporaries. Excellent.

Ludwig, Emil. *Goethe: The History of a Man*. Trans. Ethel Coburn Mayne. New York, 1928. One of the standard biographies; comprehensive in scope.

Strick, Fritz. *Goethe and World Literature*. Trans. C.A.M. Stym. London, 1949. Considers the position of Goethe in the literature of the West.

Praz, Mario. *The Romantic Agony*. Trans. Angus Davidson. New York, 1956. Psychological background. Deals with the romantic attraction to the forbidden. Essential for an understanding of romanticism.

Vietor, Karl. *Goethe the Poet.* Cambridge, Mass., 1949. Good account of the life and work of Goethe.

———. *Goethe the Thinker.* Cambridge, Mass., 1950. Considers Goethe's intellectual and philosophical orientation.

Walzel, Oskar. *German Romanticism.* Trans. Alma Elise Lussky. New York, 1932. Good philosophical-historical account of the Romantic Movement in Germany.

Wellek, Rene. *Concepts of Criticism.* Stephen G. Nichols, Jr., ed. New Haven, Conn., 1963. Excellent historical and philosophical treatment of the concepts of romanticism.

www.ingramcontent.com/pod-product-compliance
Lightning Source LLC
LaVergne TN
LVHW021716060526
838200LV00050B/2697